Made-to-Order Lean

*Excelling in a High-Mix,
Low-Volume Environment*

by Greg Lane

Foreword by

John Shook

Productivity *Press*

New York

Most Productivity Press books are available at quantity discounts when purchased in bulk. For more information, contact our Customer Service Department (888-319-5852). Address all other inquiries to:

Productivity Press
444 Park Avenue South, 7th Floor
New York, NY 10016
United States of America
Telephone: 212-686-5900
Fax: 212-686-5411
E-mail: info@productivitypress.com
ProductivityPress.com

Library of Congress Cataloging-in-Publication Data

Lane, Greg.
  Made-to-order lean : excelling in a high-mix, low-volume environment / by Greg Lane.
     p. cm.
  Includes index.
   ISBN 978-1-56327-362-9 (alk. paper)
  1. Production management. 2. Industrial efficiency. 3. Organizational effec-tiveness. I. Title.
   TS155.L2524 2007
   658.5—dc22

                                                                    2007027867

11   10   09   08   07   5   4   3   2   1

Table of Contents

Foreword

Finally, here is a practical guide to simply introduce the Toyota Production System (TPS) in job shop environments.

Experienced lean hands know that TPS was born in what had traditionally been managed as job shops, machining operations with low volume and relatively high variety. But, as Toyota grew in fortune and TPS grew in fame, the lean production application that came to be held up as the example to study is the moving conveyor line in a large vehicle assembly plant. This has caused many who work in smaller job shops to scratch their heads wondering how to apply the techniques and tools they saw on Toyota's assembly lines to their own highly variable environments.

The problem all along was that the key was not to focus on applying the tools and techniques but to apply the principles. A large, assembly plant-style Kanban system may not seem to translate directly or easily to a small job shop with hundreds or thousands of low-volume or even single-run SKUs, but the principles of Just-In-Time (producing the right part at the right time in the right amount) of building-in-quality while respecting the people who do the work certainly apply. The question managers must address is simply how to adopt and adapt the principles to make them work in different environments. The translation is more straight-forward than you might expect, but a necessary one nonetheless.

Your guide, Greg Lane, is highly qualified to help you through the translation process. Greg learned lean directly from senior Toyota Production System sensei during his stint at GM's venture with Toyota, New United Motor Manufacturing Inc. (NUMMI), as one of the fortunate few to go through highly specialized "TPS Key Person Training" at the hands of Toyota's most experienced TPS sensei in Toyota City, Japan. Following years of learning TPS in diverse settings, Greg directly managed the implementation of TPS ion his own job shop precision machining company.

If you own, manage, or work in a job shop and will simply give a try to the ideas, tools and principles described in this book, I predict you will find great success and will refer to this book over and over for years.

John Shook
The TWI Network
Ann Arbor
July 2007

Introduction: Method and Overview

The Toyota Production System (TPS) and lean principals can generally be applied to high-mix, low-volume environments, although the implementation methods are not always directly applicable. Often, the implementation process requires different methods and tools based on TPS and lean principles that will work in a high-mix environment. The proven tools and methods that are presented in this book are based on years of hands-on experience.

Within the context of this book, *"high-mix, low-volume"* refers to manufacturing businesses that have hundreds to thousands of active part numbers, with few (or none) of these parts having ongoing forecasted volumes. Orders are not predictable, and planning is safer after a firm order is in hand. This scenario applies to firms that are responsible for design and configuration of a product and to job shops that build only to order. It can also apply to companies that remanufacture or repair products.

The obvious assumption that "time is your most valuable resource" is the underlying philosophy on which everything in this book is based. In addition, all methods presented in this book assume the involvement of everyone affected during the development and implementation of the tools. By being included in the development, everyone will understand and will likely support the change; otherwise resistance is natural.

The primary foci of this book are eliminating non-value added activities (those activities that do not actually work on and transform a product) and improvements that bring immediate benefits. It is further recommended that you focus your improvements on your most repetitive jobs—your "bread and butter" work—a strategy that gives you more time to produce your low volume work or one-offs. It is assumed throughout this book that you either build to order or assemble to order and therefore rarely have influence on the production lot size. The lot size is only addressed if you decide to convert a component or finished good to *kanban*.

How to Use This Book

1. If you are aware of a specific opportunity or have an explicit business need in your high-mix plant that is covered in the scope of this book, check what is covered in each chapter in the Table of Contents or on the Implementation Flow chart at the end of this introduction and consult the relevant chapter or chapters.

2. If you are looking to make general improvements in your high-mix, low-volume business, you might find it useful to read through the entire book, noting areas that offer the most opportunity for you. It is worthwhile to first look over the Implementation Flow chart to understand how the book moves through the topics. If you believe that most of your opportunities are in your office areas, start with chapters 11 through 13; if you feel there are more improvement possibilities in the shop (given that more capital and resources are utilized there), start with chapters 1 through 10. Even if you feel that particular areas in your business are doing reasonably well, reviewing individual chapters that deal with those areas may provide some practical ideas for further improvements.

While the Implementation Flow chart is useful, it may not answer all of your questions if you are unsure whether you have a particular concept in place and are working in a lean manner. In that case, it is more productive to read the relevant chapter to acquire a better understanding of the concept and how it can be applied.

The book is organized by themes that systematically progress into other themes or areas. Note that placing the shop floor improvement chapters at the beginning of the book is not meant to indicate that these are of a higher priority, but there are often significant resources on the shop floor, and it is easier to identify and implement potential improvements there before branching into other areas. Moreover, in low-volume business, there is often a final assembly process that is supplied by upstream processes and purchased components. Typically the right parts do not show up for assembly when they are required; in these cases it is best to start lean implementation in the shop. As getting all the parts to the necessary point on time is one of the greatest difficulties in low volume and requires an understanding of lead time and robust planning systems, those issues will be addressed in these chapters. In high-mix, low-volume environments, you frequently have proportionally more resources in the office than in a high-volume plant, so you want to consider the office-improvement chapters if that scenario applies to you.

This book is meant to help lean practitioners who find it difficult to apply lean principals in low-volume plants. It does not cover any of the following:

- Quality techniques (the author assumes you already have a reasonable quality level)
- Problem-solving methods
- An explanation of why you need to change to a lean culture or start implementing lean (this is a guide book on how to do it, not why)
- An introduction or history of basic lean concepts
- How to manage change or manage people

Because some lean terminology and industrial acronyms help to simplify the discussion, they are used in this book; a glossary is provided at the end of the text to help with any unfamiliar terms. One important point to clarify in this introductory section is the distinction between lean and Six Sigma. In general terms, lean is the reduction of waste while Six Sigma is the reduction of variation. Because Six Sigma is based on statistical methods to help in problem solving, it can be difficult to apply in high-mix, low-volume environments because you rarely repeat the same processes enough to apply statistical methods. The same problem will not be observed with enough frequency to effectively utilize this technique.

Each business is different, so it is all but impossible to recommend an implementation sequence that will work in all cases. The Implementation Flow Chart at the end of this introduction tries to show, for example, that if your quality is not stable, this should be your first concern. After that, you want to have your capacity balanced with your demand before working to reduce costs. In the office, it is better to look at entire departments for improvement before targeting specific office processes. A few additional general items to keep in mind when introducing change within an organization are listed below:

- Any time you introduce change to a process involving an operator, there is a temporary negative effect while the operator learns the new process. After a short learning curve, the benefit will be evident.

- You should always concentrate first on improving non-value-added work (inventories, getting tools and materials, transporting work, walking) because it rarely involves investment. Improving value-added work is more likely to involve investment.

- Each department should work to improve its processes and clarify what it is capable of doing, instead of pointing out problems perceived to be caused by other departments.

- Within a high-mix plant, the production system should be process focused instead of product focused.

- It is too easy to improve a process and not change the manager's focus or support for this new or improved process. For this reason, standardized work for managers is encouraged as one of the first steps.

- If you do not currently have a measurement system for improvements, you will need one, especially for tracking productivity and lead time.

- If managers are not able to perform the jobs of everyone they supervise and understand how to apply a scientific method of problem solving, they will be less effective in leading change.

Because the chapters of this book are grouped by themes, there are some lean techniques that cross into multiple chapters. Therefore, one chapter will explain how to apply a particular method in a low-volume environment, and other chapters will cross-reference this explanation. Given space constraints, it is more important to discuss how a particular method can be adapted to a low-volume environment than it is to try to include a detailed explanation that is readily available elsewhere. Thus, although some methods may be described only briefly, readers will be directed to references that provide more detailed information. The ideas and methods presented here are based on common sense, and this is why they are successful. You may be surprised how much opportunity you find, so it is best to concentrate only on what your organization truly needs and is capable of implementing.

Prior to starting any lean implementation or using the various techniques presented in this book, you should first have a vision as to where you want to go with lean and what your expectations are. Second, you want to develop the skills needed for lean implementation within your organization. The third requirement is to provide a reason or incentive to change. Finally, you need an action plan, one that has clear actions with defined measurements. Once the incentive(s) and action plan(s) are clearly communicated to the organization and once you have buy-in from the workforce, you are ready to proceed.

If you find that you or others do not have the commitment or faith to proceed on a grand scale, begin on a smaller scale. Choose one of the chapters that discusses a lot of opportunity for improvement and implement an enhancement that will be a "quick win." It will be easier to get people on board and interested in other projects once they see an initial success.

High-Mix/Low-Volume Implementation Flow Chart

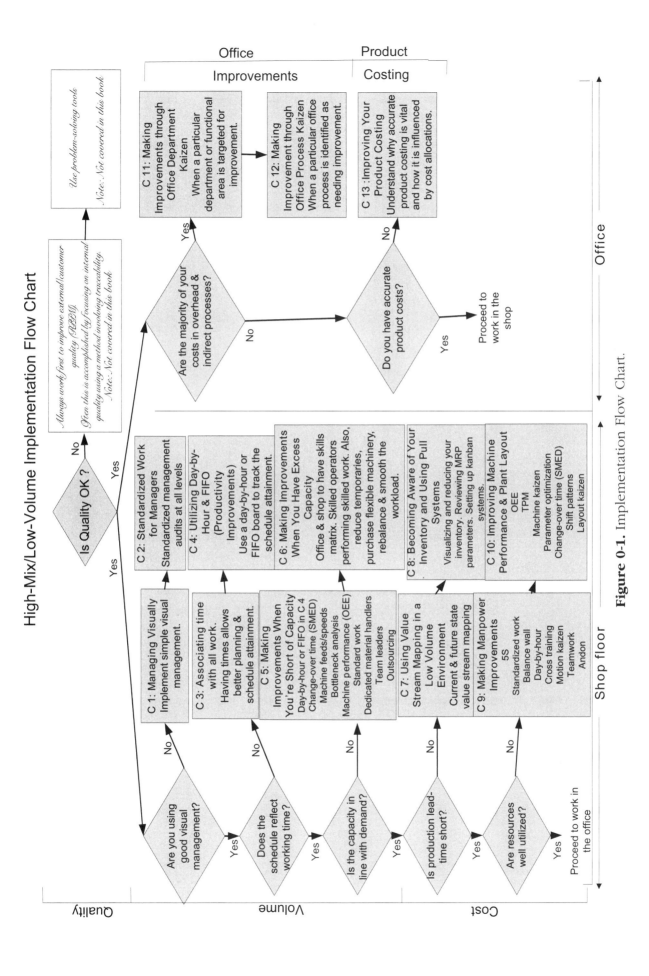

Figure 0-1. Implementation Flow Chart.

1

Managing Visually

Visualization is an important starting point for managing in real time, either on the shop floor or in the department where the work is being completed. If you cannot clearly and quickly understand the status of your system, you will have a hard time prioritizing your limited resources. Putting simple visualization systems in place helps you in developing an eye for waste or at least pushes you into asking specific questions and getting to the root cause of problems.

What gets measured usually improves, yet many companies are content to perform financial measurements at a high level within the company. Activity on the shop floor is assumed to mean the area is productive, yet that activity is rarely measured directly. Even if everyone in the organization has well-developed eyes for waste and knows how to bring such waste to the attention of management, quick visualization systems allow you to manage in real time, not in a production meeting after the fact. Although there may be comfort in discussing waste in the meeting room the day after, by that point, capacity is already lost, and it can never be regained.

Visual management (also called *visuals*) allows you to quickly grasp the current situation in real time. It comes in many forms: business or project plans; standardized work; schedules; production performance charts; shadow boards; value stream maps; andon signals; and so on. Although there is a fine line between "visual management" and "industrial wallpaper," if you do not create a lean foundation on the shop floor and construct useful visuals, you have wasted your time.

When developing any visual, you need to involve everyone who will either supply information or utilize the available information. Explain the reasons for the visual and get feedback and buy-in. This chapter first focuses on ensuring you are measuring the correct items, and then shows you how to utilize the best visual format on your shop floor and in your office.

Using the Right Metrics

Metrics (also known as *performance indicators*) are measurements used to determine whether a process is improving. Often, metrics are based on quality, productivity, cost, delivery, profitability, and safety. Good metrics are aligned through the organization in the form of strategic planning, starting from the corporation's goals, which are then linked to the plant's goals and then further linked to each department's goals.

Before discussing how visual management is implemented most effectively in the office and factory, be sure your management is using the right measurements to drive improvements. All measurements drive behavior, and the wrong measurements can cause negative effects. Financial performance measures record history whereas nonfinancial numbers can measure in real time and can be traced directly to financial results.

Traditional "management by objectives" taught in business schools can be dangerous since it recommends performance be measured by quality, inventory, customer service, profit, labor efficiency, overhead costs, machine utilization, etc., when in fact improving one of these measures can drag down another and confuse management. Lean instead focuses its measures on improving the flow of materials and information, knowing this will improve performance.

Since we need measures to understand if we are improving, ask yourself: Does the metric measure what is important, and does it drive the correct behavior? When reviewing visuals, be clear about who is responsible for this chart/measurement, know what it is actually measuring, and make sure your metric does not fall into one of the following three categories:

1. **The responsible manager has little influence.** Understand how the metric is calculated and what influence the responsible person has over the factors in the equation. Assuming the metric consists of a numerator and denominator, does the manager have influence over one or both? Consider, for example, a production manager who is responsible for a productivity measurement of "wages/sales." In many cases, a production manager is not able to directly influence wages (although he or she might have a small influence regarding overtime), because there is a fixed number of permanent employees at predetermined wages. Sales figures are usually the responsibility of the sales department; therefore, the production manager has little influence (he or she can try only to get all orders shipped by the request date). However, if you change the metric to "minutes/part," there is direct accountability, which should push the production

manager to improve productivity. It is advisable to review your metrics and determine whether the responsible manager(s) actually has a direct influence over the factors comprising the measurement.

2. **Metrics are subject to opinions or outside factors.** RPPM (returned parts per million) is an example of an important and necessary measurement, but it often represents the customer's inspection/perception. There is also usually a delay in obtaining and acting on this data, and some customer complaints are either outside the internal inspection limits or are caused by outside factors (for example, shipping damage, improper application, and so on). So although this metric must be looked at and all returns must be analyzed, it is sometimes better for the quality and production managers to track and base immediate actions on internal quality measures rather than quality issues that make it through to customers. (Also, internal quality should measure and reflect the types of RPPMs being discovered and should periodically be adjusted to reflect the customer's quality concerns.)

3. **Measurements encourage behavior not in line with lean thinking.** A classic example of a poor productivity measurement is "efficiency" (that is, hours utilized/total hours available), because this drives you to keep machines and people busy, not necessarily manufacturing what is needed when it is needed (as is done with just-in-time [JIT] manufacturing).

Some Recommended Metrics

Try to avoid any measures with the three characteristics discussed in the preceding section. Using the following recommended metrics, which are in line with lean philosophies, is a better approach. Remember if you are measuring specific processes with a metric, you should begin at the bottleneck.

Quality:

First time quality = units passed without rework/total units produced

Cost of poor quality = total cost (labor and material) associated with rework and scrap

Productivity and cost:

Productivity = minutes/part

Productivity = pieces/hour

OEE (overall equipment effectiveness) = Availability × Performance × Quality

Absorption of standard hours (if you use standard hours and trust them; *standard hours* are the number of hours a skilled worker would take to complete a given job without encountering problems. Standard hours are computed by using time-and-motion studies and are used as a measurement in standard costing)

Customer service:

Core products delivered within lead time/total requested

Service parts delivered within lead time/total requested

Inventory:

Days Supply Inventory (DSI) = total stock value/sales per day (use a sales average)

Note: Customer service and inventory can have an inverse correlation; therefore management must balance the goals between them

Profitability (a historical measure):

Use standard return on investment (ROI: the income that an investment provides in a year) and net earnings (NE: gross sales minus taxes, depreciation, interest, and other expenses)

Safety:

Recordables = number of incidents causing lost work days

First aid = number of incidents, first aid treatment, or near misses

Characteristics of Poor Visuals

Typical characteristics of poor visuals are listed below. An illustration is provided in Figure 1-1.

- It's unclear who is responsible in the visual.
- The metrics goal is unclear, or hasn't been given a lot of thought.
- It is reviewed infrequently, or not at all.
- The visual gives too much information.
- It is unclear how data is calculated or where data comes from.
- The major influences on the measurement are unsure.
- There are no actions shown; or the actions are without status or expected outcomes.

Characteristics of Good Visuals

This section outlines typical characteristics of good visuals. Figures 1-2, 1-3, and 1-4 provide illustrations for the concepts listed below.

- The name of the person or group responsible is assigned to each metric.
- The metric represents a clear goal, is well thought out (for example, is adjusted for seasonal factors), and targets particular improvements.

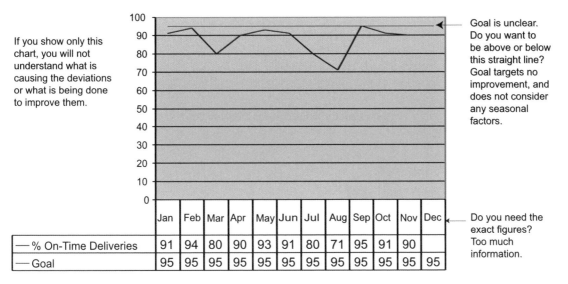

Figure 1-1. Poor visual.

- The metric is reviewed regularly by appropriate managers.

- The visual is easy to read (it takes only a few seconds to grasp the situation).

- Everyone can understand how the measurement is calculated.

- The visual clearly indicates which major value streams, products, and/or areas influence the particular metric (a value stream consists of all the

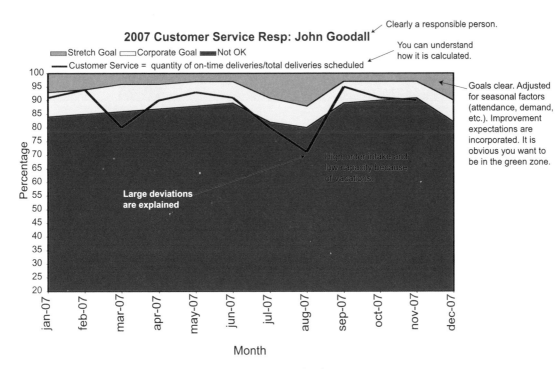

Figure 1-2. A good visual of customer service.

value-added and non-value-added work required to develop and produce a product).

- Everyone can understand the current actions, their status, and the expected outcome.
- The visual can be easily kept up to date (with a pencil, if possible).

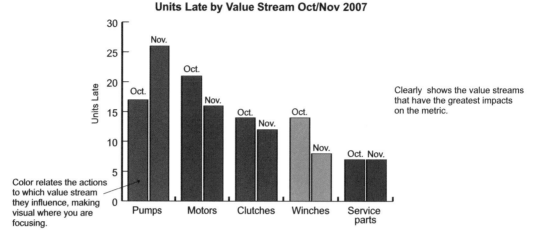

Figure 1-3. Areas influencing customer service.

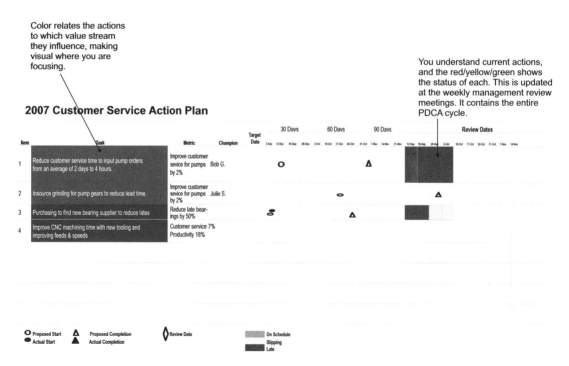

Figure 1-4. Action plan to improve customer service.

Note: Prior to a weekly review meeting, each person responsible for an action colors the review box corresponding to the week with either a red, yellow, or green highlighter: red if it appears that the target date will not be achieved; yellow if the action is behind schedule but might still meet the target date; and green if the action is on schedule or nearly so. With this color-coded review box in hand, the manager hosting the meeting does not need to waste time discussing actions that are green and can focus on helping to get the yellow and red actions back on track.

Four Types of Visual Boards

Four major types of visual boards—office boards, plant boards, value stream boards, and team boards—are discussed in the following sections.

Office Boards

An *office board* is a visual board used in a department like purchasing, engineering, finance, human resources, or administration (but not on the production floor). Ideally, each department has its measurements and goals; therefore, a visual board is used so that an entire department can participate in improvements and other departments understand the areas of focus and how those improvements may affect them.

The example in Figure 1-5 is a chart for an engineering department responsible for configuring systems for newly received orders. The engineers determined that if there is a queue of more then ten orders waiting, they are in jeopardy of delay; more then twenty orders waiting will definitely delay manu-

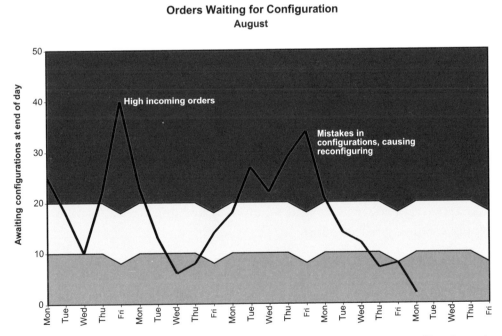

Figure 1-5. Example of a chart partially comprising a complete office board.

facturing's start date. Notice that the goal is adjusted to take into account a shorter working day on Fridays.

Plant Boards

A *plant board* is used in the production area, but it represents all the value streams within an entire plant. It is a very important tool not only for managing the business from the shop floor, but also to drive and measure improvements. On this board, you are usually working with monthly data, but weekly data should be used wherever possible, as weekly meetings should be conducted at this board with timely data. A working definition of a plant board is presented on pages 10 and 11, along with the differences between successful boards and others that merely present information without a related purpose.

A plant board should tell you at a glance where you stand on the important measures and whether your actions are having an impact and are being completed on time. Using colors is a quick and easy way to ensure people understand the status. Remember that, in addition to the plant board, you might also have value stream and team boards, depending on the size and type of your plant, the products you make, and how management responsibilities are divided. The most important point of a plant board is to serve as a working tool, not simply a display of information. It not only shows the goals and results for your metrics but also helps pinpoint which areas (or value streams) are having the most negative impact on productivity and helps to assign responsibility and actions to reach desired goals.

The board should be set up with no more than five or six metrics (usually one for each category), listed in descending order of importance. For example, some companies state that safety is their overriding priority, so "safety" should be listed at the top. Earnings may be next, followed by quality (first-time internal quality), customer service (percent on-time deliveries), and so forth.

One number that affects all metrics is sales. It is hard to understand the development of individual metrics without knowing whether sales increased or decreased during the same period; therefore, it is best to put a sales graph at the top of the board (this is not normally followed by a Pareto chart or action list unless your sales department is being managed from the plant board). Naturally, the type of products sold and when they are due needs to be a consideration when creating a sales graph.

In Figure 1-6, Plant Board 1 is a working tool for the plant: It displays results; makes analysis; and plans, assigns, and tracks ongoing actions. Figure 1-7 is a display on which management communicates results, but it does not indicate what influences the measurement or what is being done to improve it. There is also an overwhelming amount of information that requires some time to understand; it is probably not read by the operators and was likely designed by someone with a technical background.

For each measurement, an owner should be assigned. The owner is not responsible for implementing all the improvements for this metric; he or she is responsible for the metric reaching its target and following up with others involved in implementing the tasks that affect the metric. Obviously, the owner should be a high-level person within the organization; many companies even connect this metric with personal annual goals and objectives set forth in annual evaluations.

If a detailed and precise numerical metric cannot be displayed on the shop floor because of its sensitive nature, the actual numbers may be represented by a ratio or percentage (for example, earnings use relative net earnings [NE] without labeling the axis or use return on investment). The actual number can also be divided by a factor that is known only to management.

Once you have your metrics and their respective owners displayed on the board, everyone can quickly grasp the situation. Color-coded graphs make it easy to see what should increase or decrease, what is acceptable, and what requires attention and improvement. Nobody wants to be in the red because red signifies that a problem exists. You can also show two separate target areas, such as a corporate target (which could be the yellow zone) and a tougher plant goal (which could be the green area). If you only have one target, the yellow zone can be set up as 5 percent or 10 percent above or below the green zone.

A goal that is drawn as a level line (without an increasing or decreasing slope) can be problematic, because it is usually unrealistic. Refer to Figure 1-1, in which the manager has set a customer service goal of 97 percent on-time deliveries for the entire year, yet no improvements have been targeted, no high-order intake periods have been considered, and no seasonal factors have been taken into account. A good example of how goals and metrics can complement one another can be seen in European companies, many of which have reduced sales in August and December because of holidays and shutdowns. They anticipate how this will affect a particular metric and set their goals accordingly (refer to Figure 1-2). In addition, because most metrics are reached by making many small improvements, the goal should increase or decrease over a period of time in small increments instead of being a level line that is reassessed and changed once a year. As a rule, whenever the goal increases or decreases, there should be a business or market reason.

It is always good to show exactly how the metric is calculated so that everyone has a clear understanding of what affects it. Never assume that the calculation of the metric is obvious to everyone, because most companies have a slightly different definition of the same metric.

Plant Board (left side only)

Stockton Plant

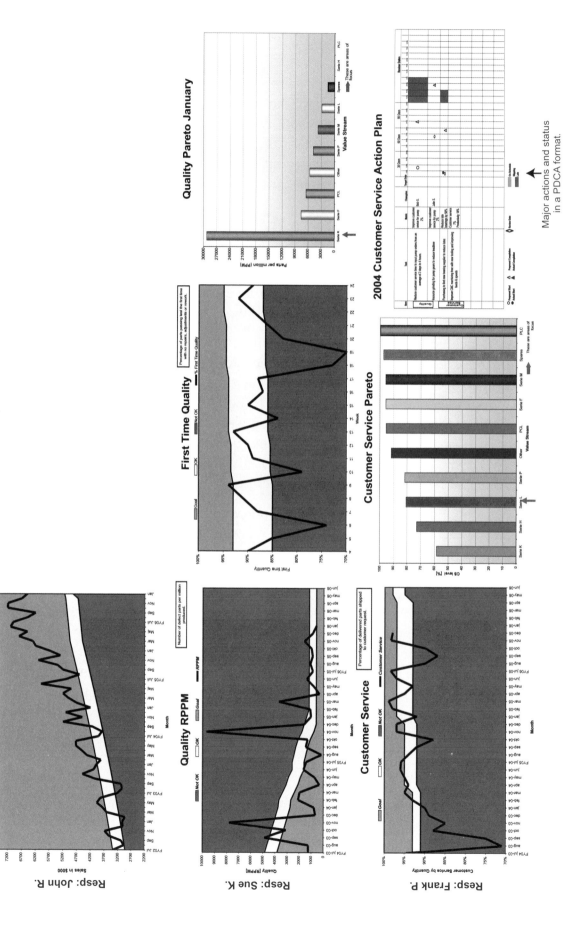

10

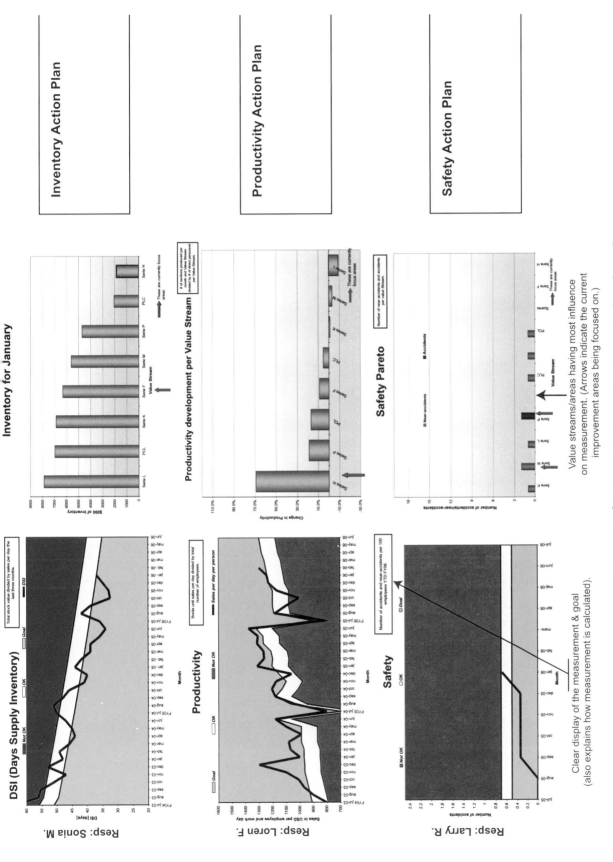

Figure 1-6. Example of a well-designed plant board.

11

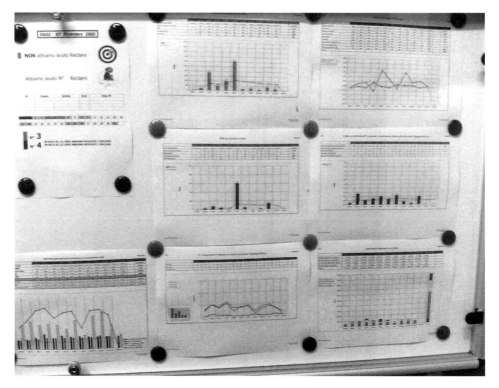

Figure 1-7. Example of a poorly devised plant board.

Pareto Charts

Each metric is affected by different areas of the plant, different products, or different processes. A *Pareto chart* shows which area or product has the most influence on a metric. This type of chart is the bar graph shown to the right of each line graph (as in Plant Board 1 in Figure 1-6), and the first bar always indicates the value stream or product having the most influence on the metric. For example, customer service is a number this company wants to increase; therefore, the product with the lowest percentage of customer service is the priority for improvement (unless this product accounts only for a low sales volume). On the other hand, RPPM is a number this company wants to decrease; therefore, the product lines with the highest value are on the left of the Pareto chart because they offer the most opportunities. The arrow under a particular value stream on the Pareto chart shows clearly where you are concentrating your improvement activities.

Action Plans

The next chart to the left (shown only for customer service on Plant Board 1 in Figure 1-6) is a task list in which the tasks are shaded the same color as the bars (or product lines) they will help to improve. These *action plans* are the high-level tasks associated with each respective metric; the more specific tasks will be on the value stream and team boards. Action plans make it easy to see how many actions are related to a bar on the Pareto chart (which represents an area or product in the plant). On the right side of the action plan (where you see the red/yellow/green boxes filled in) is where the responsible person updates his or her progress each week. This is a timesaving strategy for managers—green-colored actions signify an action is on schedule and does not require a review.

The plant board is read from top to bottom, and then from left to right. Read down the list of metrics until you reach one in the red zone. Then look to the right to see which product areas have the most influence over this metric. Then look at the actions being taken and whether the person responsible is on schedule. Always compare each metric to the sales graph (at the top of the board), because it has a direct correlation to most measurements.

Other Items to Display

A few other items (not shown in Figure 1-6) should also be displayed on the right side of the plant board. The current and future state site layout, for example, helps show how physical changes will improve flow, and what characteristics you consider important in improving flow. An analysis showing your progress on implementing lean is also helpful.

The plant board is reviewed by the plant manager and value stream managers, but will usually lead to more specific reviews on the value stream and possibly the team boards.

Therefore, once you are using the right metrics and have analysis with Pareto charts, you can decide which metric to work on and use the plant board to suggest tools (discussed later in this book) to help make improvements.

Value Stream Boards

Value streams are about focusing on managing by product or customer instead of managing departmentally (e.g., press, paint, welding, assembly departments). Managing by value streams has the following advantages:

- Looks at the entire picture
- Focuses on customer or product instead of only on department
- Gives clear quality and cost responsibility of products
- Gives better understanding of complete customer requirements

A value stream board is similar to the plant board, but deals only with the flow through a particular value stream. It should be updated weekly and managed by the value stream manager. Weekly meetings should be held to review the following:

- Do the 90-day action plans relate to improvement ideas from the value stream maps?

- Are these actions going to reduce the lead time from the current state?
- Are these actions improving or going to improve the value stream metrics?
- Are the assigned people for each action on target?
- Are these actions related to customer priorities and those tasks measured on the plant board?
- Is everything being kept up to date?

Figure 1-8 gives us an example of a value stream board. Some companies track more than three metrics on this board (shown down the left side of the board), but you should track only what you feel is appropriate and manageable. Link individual actions on the action list directly to the expected improvement, which should also be tracked on the board. For example, the lower-right corner shows how many bearings arrived late each week, a measure that should improve when purchasing uses a new supplier for bearings. Ensure that weekly meetings are held and the aforementioned questions are answered.

Team Boards

A *team board* is updated daily and tracks only what is within a team's control. A team is normally a small group of people (five to ten operators) who perform similar functions. The board is updated by the team leader daily and usually tracks the detailed progress of quality (or problems in the area), productivity, on-time orders (schedule attainment), attendance, and so on. (Figure 1-9 on page 18 shows an example of a team board.) Real-time Pareto charts are a simple way to accomplish this. They are easy to develop in Microsoft Excel, but only the outline should come from a computer; data should always be filled in with a pencil and should show the biggest problems in real time to help the team leader stay focused on what is important.

Visuals to Emphasize Abnormal Conditions

There are many uses for visual management in addition to the ones already discussed in this chapter. Whenever it becomes difficult to distinguish "normal" from "abnormal," consider whether this distinction is significant to the organization and then find a simple method to show what occurs when you are operating abnormally.

A simple example is sending items outside for external processing and then having those items returned to the plant for further processing in your value stream (for example, your machined parts need external plating before you assemble them). If these items are often not returned on schedule, and if this abnormality is difficult to see, you might start a subcontractor tracking board, see Figure 1-10 on page 19.

Visual management does not need to be in the form of a chart, and you might want to consider other alternatives. If, for example, you consistently want to have a minimum of two pieces of work-in-process between machines, you can paint the floor or shelf red where the pieces would normally go. When the two pieces are not in place, the red color will stand out as an abnormality.

Red, yellow, and green provide excellent visual signals; the color scheme concept has many practical uses and works the same virtually anywhere in the world.

Summary of Key Points

- Ensure you are using the best metrics to drive improvements and that those being held accountable have influence over those metrics.
- Use a plant board as a tool to help everyone understand the current state versus management expectations, what areas or products have the most influence on a metric, what is being done at the plant level to improve each metric, and who is responsible.
- Use value stream and team boards to track weekly and daily improvements, respectively.
- The boards discussed for use on the shop floor should progress to smaller focus areas and shorter time frames (for example, the plant board focuses monthly or weekly, the value stream board focuses weekly, and the team board focuses on daily measurements).
- Remember to clarify (and standardize) who is responsible for each section of the visual.
- Standardizing the use of red, yellow, and green in your plant makes the "abnormal" situation easy to spot quickly.

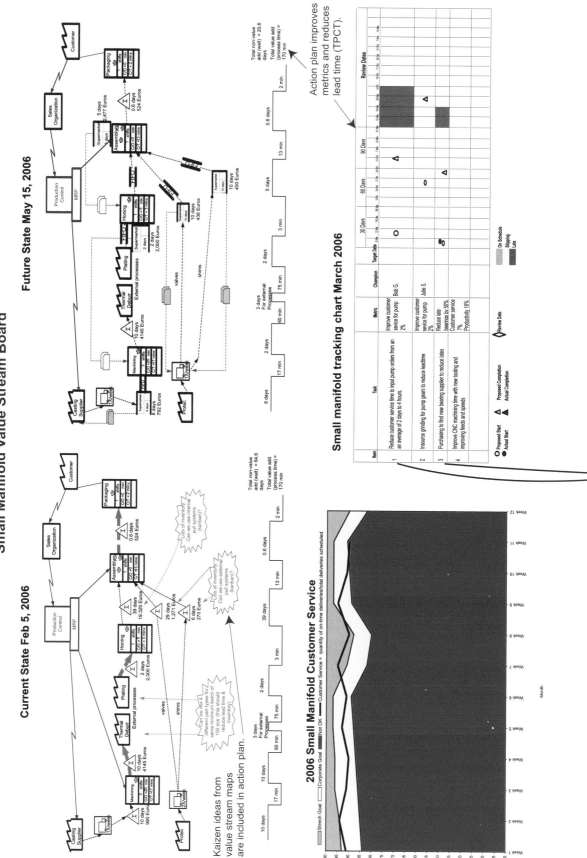

Small Manifold Value Stream Board

Future State May 15, 2006

Current State Feb 5, 2006

Total non-value add (wait) = 64.6 days

Total value add (process time) = 170 min

Total non-value add (wait) = 20.6 days

Total value add (process time) = 170 min

Action plan improves metrics and reduces lead time (TPCT).

Kaizen ideas from value stream maps are included in action plan.

Small manifold tracking chart March 2006

Item	Task	Metric	Champion	Target Date	30 Days	60 Days	90 Days	Review Dates
1	Reduce customer service time to input pump orders from an an average of 2 days to 4 hours.	Improve customer service for pump 2%	Bob G.					
2	Insource grinding for pump gears to reduce leadtime	Improve customer service for pump 2%	Julie S.					
3	Purchasing to find new bearing supplier to reduce lates	Reduce late bearings by 50%						
4	Improve CNC machining time with new tooling and improving feeds and speeds	Customer service 7% Productivity 18%						

Proposed Start ○ Proposed Completion △

Actual Start ● Actual Completion ▲

Review Date ◇

On Schedule / Slipping / Late

2006 Small Manifold Customer Service

Customer Service = quantity of on-time deliveries/total deliveries scheduled

Stretch Goal / Corporate Goal / Not OK

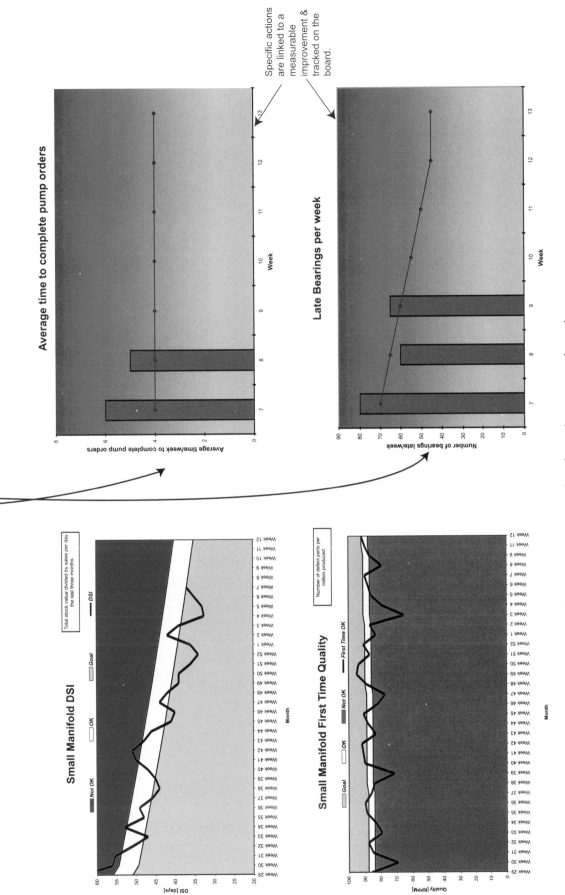

Figure 1-8. Example of a value stream board.

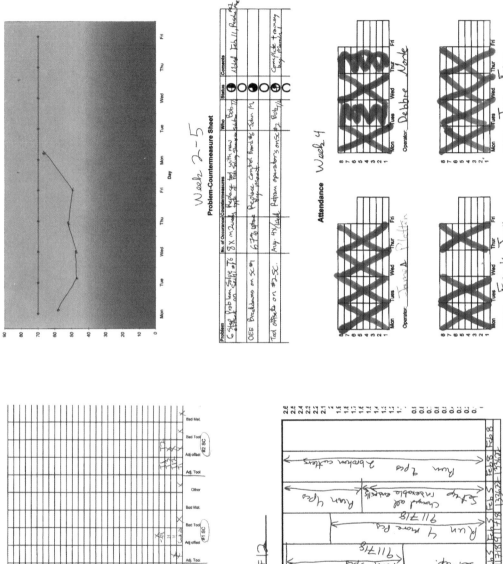

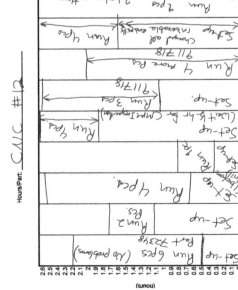

Figure 1-9. Example of a team board.

Subcontractor Tracking Board

Work Order	Supplier	Date Sent	Date Expected	Actual Date Received
13354	A-1 Plating	4-Jan	7-Jan	10-Jan
24456	John's Heat Treat	6-Jan	13-Jan	13-Jan
21134	A-1 Plating	7-Jan	12-Jan	
32212	City Painting	7-Jan	14-Jan	

Figure 1-10. Subcontractor tracking board.

Color Examples of Red, Yellow, and Green Visuals from Other Chapters

Orders Waiting for Configuration
August

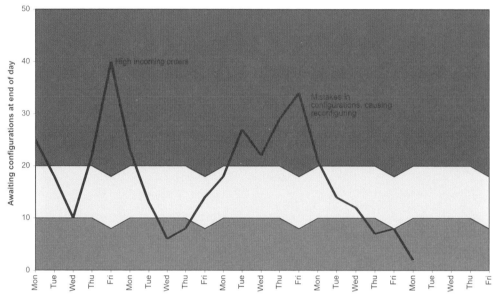

Figure 4-1. Monitoring and improving office productivity.

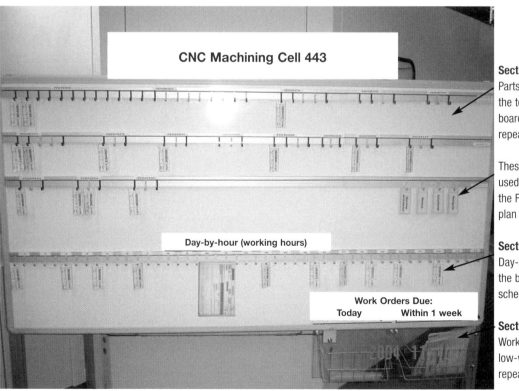

Figure 4-8. A combined kanban and work-order board that includes day-by-hour.

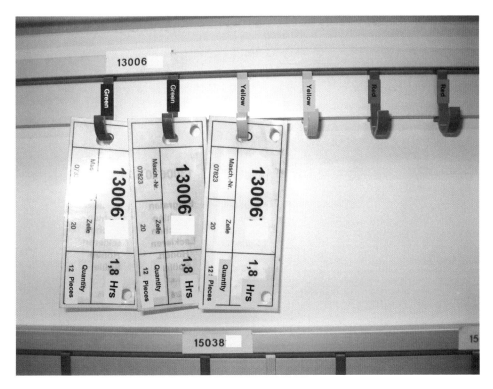

Figure 4-10. Kanban cards on board.

Skills Matrix - Purchasing Department

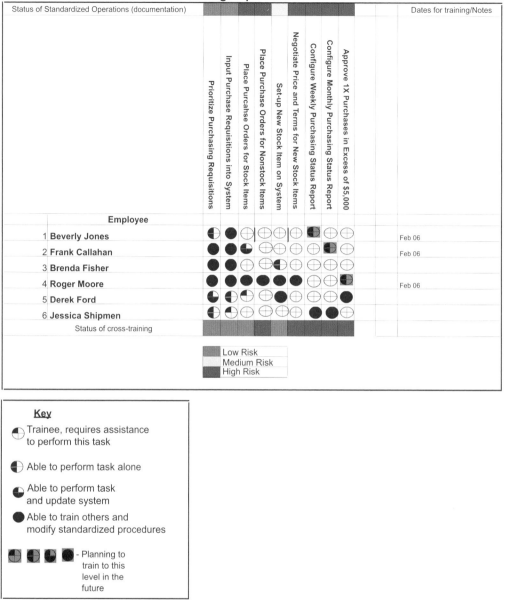

Figure 6-2. Skills matrix for a purchasing department.

Figure 8-6. Kanban board.

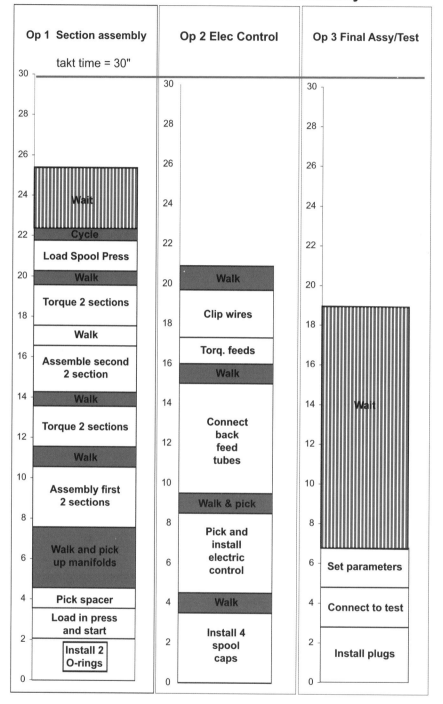

Figure 9-7. Operator balance wall example for a manifold assembly cell.

Figure 9-8. Light bar with sound module added on.

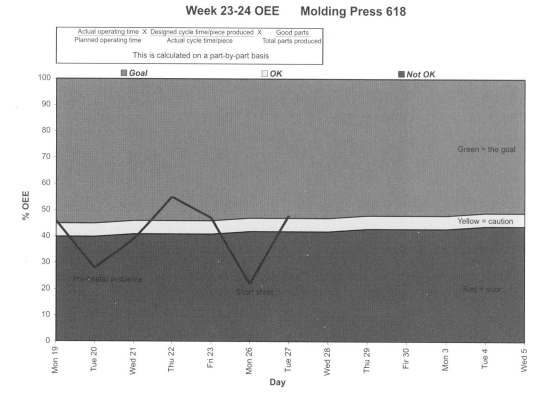

Figure 10-1. OEE tracking with a clearly defined goal and calculation method.

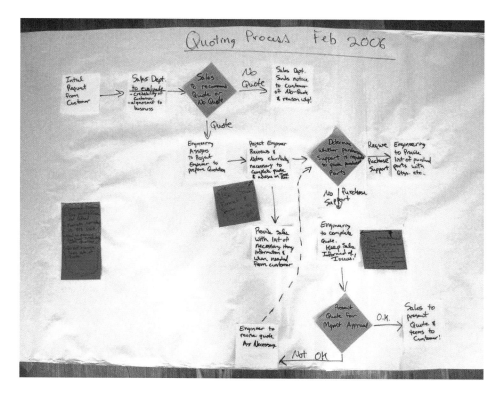

Figure 11-6. Process map using sticky-back notes.

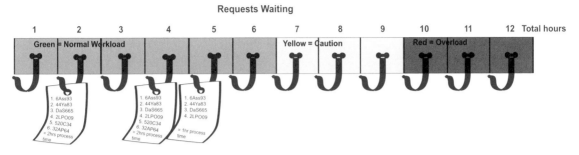

Figure 12-2. Visualizing when purchasing might exceed wait time.

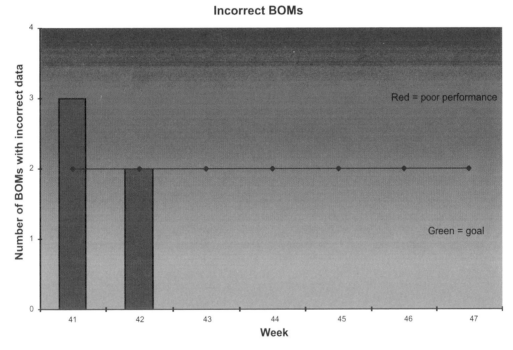

Figure 12-4. Setting a target and tracking the success of each action.

2

Management Auditing: Standardized Work for Managers

Managers must continuously verify a business and its processes. This oversight involves not only shopfloor audits, but also visiting the supporting departments. Naturally, it is much easier to understand the status and identify opportunities if good visual management is in place (see chapter 1), but too much visual management can sometimes create new problems. At certain management levels, specifically those with a large scope of responsibility, the task of continuous visual checking for areas that should be audited seems overwhelming. This is particularly true when an organization is in the process of going lean. But this surface perception of an increased auditing workload, accompanied by numerous review meetings, is false. With lean, there should be less time spent in meetings and more time spent reviewing the various processes. Moreover, good visual management makes it easier (and, therefore, quicker) to audit processes—if the auditing process itself is sound and if it is rationally scheduled as a part of management activities.

It is vitally important to have a certain time set aside for auditing and to have a logical method, a type of standardized work, that managers can use. There should be a sacred time for this each day, with an audit schedule and a standard set of questions or review points to keep the audit focused. A robust auditing process by managers is very important: Once this process is in place, productivity improvements will become the norm. As this chapter will demonstrate, the auditing process need not be complicated or difficult.

Building an Audit Schedule

Auditing is one of the most important functions in any lean company and is critical to the change process. Many companies put new tools/processes in place and expect associates to change without requiring management to change. One of the important changes that managers must make is to restructure their daily activities to accommodate and drive the auditing process.

Depending on the level of management involved, many items should be checked on a daily or weekly basis. Because some audits will involve more than one manager, it is better for everyone to decide collectively whether mornings or afternoons are better for the reviews. This approach allows management to plan meetings and other events that synchronize with, rather than disrupt, audit time. To simplify this scheduling, have everyone involved complete a simple weekly calendar. Note that all of these individual calendars should be in the same format, because this will facilitate finding common times.

MANAGER'S WEEKLY CALENDAR					
	Monday	Tuesday	Wednesday	Thursday	Friday
07:30 – 08:00					
08:00 – 08:30	Production startup	Production startup	Production startup	Production startup	Production startup
08:30 – 09:00					
09:00 – 09:30					
09:30 – 10:00			Proposed Audit Time		
10:00 – 10:30					
10:30 – 11:00					
11:00 – 11:30	Purchasing meeting				
11:30 – 12:00					
12:00 – 12:30					
12:30 – 13:00					
13:00 – 13:30			Planning review	Interviews	
13:30 – 14:00	Shift planning			Interviews	
14:00 – 14:30				Interviews	Weekly reporting
14:30 – 15:00				Interviews	
15:00 – 15:30				Interviews	
15:30 – 16:00				Interviews	
16:00 – 16:30					
16:30 – 17:00					

Figure 2-1. Example of a manager's schedule with a proposed auditing time.

Figure 2-1 shows what should be prepared prior to the managers sitting together to decide on a sacred time for audits. The other needed data is a list of items to be audited, and in what frequency. Input should come from managers as well as staff. Lean managers or support persons should also be asked for input. Managers can prepare a simple task list in a simple-to-follow format like the one shown in Figure 2-2.

Who: **PRODUCTION MANAGER**

Task	Frequency			Method	Materials needed
	daily	weekly	monthly		
Visual board audits	verify daily	per schedule		Lean manager to prepare schedule of areas and pre-audit	Audit method and questions to be prepared by lean manager. Each board may require a different method, depending on its purpose.
5S audit		per schedule		Lean manager to prepare schedule of areas and pre-audit	Standard 5S audit sheet
TPM		per schedule		Lean manager to prepare schedule of areas and pre-audit	Standard TPM audit sheet
Capacity Planning Board	verify daily			Check production control's board daily to see customer requirements & compare to capacity	Available production capacity plan for the next week
Accounting board audit			1X/ month	Plant manager, production manager, production control manager, accounting manager, and end of month review	Audit sheet to review key financial numbers and detailed Paretos showing value streams having most effect.

Figure 2-2. Proposed audit task list and schedule.

Looking at an Example

After these planning meetings, develop an audit schedule and standardized audit sheets.

Figure 2-3 shows an example of a final weekly audit schedule. Each day has a specific theme and targets a predetermined department. This schedule may be published, or it can be kept secret so that departments cannot prepare for the audit. The managers conducting the audit, however, should involve the lean champion (if one is available) and the responsible supervisor.

For each type of audit, you also want to have a specific checklist so that managers are focused and utilize a standardized approach. Figure 2-4 is an example; it shows a list of tasks or focus items, each of which can be rated on a scale of 0 to 5. The checklist includes a column for comments where an explanation for a low rating or additional information can be inserted. It might take some time to develop a consensus for what constitutes a 1 versus a 2 rating or a 4 versus a 5 rating, but this is part of the developmental process and is usually shaped by a company's (or department's) particular needs.

	Monday	Tuesday	Wednesday	Thursday	Friday
Week 1	Visual Mgmt Pre-machining	Schedule Attainment Frame fabrication	Inventory Review Rotor machining	Workplace Org. - 5S Rotor assembly	Problem Solving Frame assembly
Week 2	Visual Mgmt Final assembly	Schedule Attainment Engineering	Inventory Review Purchasing	Workplace Org. - 5S Pre-machining	Problem Solving Frame fabrication
Week 3	Visual Mgmt Rotor machining	Schedule Attainment Frame assembly	Inventory Review Final Assembly	Workplace Org. - 5S Engineering	Problem Solving Purchasing
Week 4	Visual Mgmt Frame fabrication	Schedule Attainment Pre-machining	Inventory Review Rotor assembly	Workplace Org. - 5S Rotor machining	Problem Solving Final assembly
Week 5	Visual Mgmt Engineering	Schedule Attainment Rotor machining	Inventory Review Frame fabrication	Workplace Org. - 5S Purchasing	Problem Solving Pre-machining

Figure 2-3. Final audit schedule.

	Date:	Feb 3		Comments
	Scale	0–5	0–5	
Unnecessary items removed from area		2		
Parts storage is organized & labeled		3		
All parts are stored in designated place		3		
Standard WIP as noted by visuals		2		
All parts in the correct quantity		1		
Foot printing for all appropriate items		1		
Shadow boards in place & utilized		2		
Air lines off the floor & stored properly		1		
Dustpans & brooms in designated areas		2		
Floor free & clean		3		
Equipment clean		2		
Standard documentation (posted & current)		1		*Needs board bolted up, currently on floor*

Key: 0 = no evidence   1 = started   2 = three items out of std.   3 = two items out of std.   4 = one item out std.   5 = excellent

Figure 2-4. Checksheet.

Use the checksheets as an integral, ongoing part of the review/audit process. Once the initial audit is completed, post the filled-in audit checksheet in the area. The next time you audit the area, review the last audit checksheet to ensure the comments made at that time have been addressed.

Summary of Key Points

- Standardized audits turn weak managers into stronger managers.

- You cannot become lean by putting any new tool (especially visual management) in place without standardizing management audits of these visuals.

- You cannot expect the organization to change its behavior and working method without the managers changing their methods.

- All managers should prepare an individual weekly calendar and a recommended audit schedule before getting together to develop a plant wide audit schedule.

- If managers do not follow the audit schedule, they send the wrong message to the organization: that visual management is not important.

3

Associating a Time
with All Work

"Associating a time" does not mean that you need serious industrial engineering in your low-volume operation—after all, who has time for that? But all products need a price and are, therefore, linked to time. In other words, time is money! Any target, indicating how long something should take, is better than no target. For this to be beneficial, however, you must measure your actual time against the targeted time. The following are some benefits of associating a time with each job:

- Ability to schedule
- Productivity increase of 10 percent to 15 percent if visually comparing planned versus actual time using a *day-by-hour chart* (in which predetermined hourly production targets are visually tracked; see chapter 4)
- Improved product costing
- Ability to confirm accuracy of estimates

In high-mix, low-volume plants and job shops, work is usually scheduled on the shop floor only in terms of customer priorities or dates. In many plants, a schedule is developed to indicate which jobs should be completed in which order, but specific time schedules are rarely given and even rarer is the concept of continuous monitoring and problem elimination. This is like running your business by giving everyone a blank check: "Just let me know whenever you complete that work order, and I will give you the next job." A much better way to approach your target needs is, "According to the estimated time (or standard hours or historical timing), you should complete this work order by 09:30 and start on the next; please let me know if you begin encountering problems."

I have rarely encountered a business where there is not some sort of expectation as to how long some process should take to complete, whether based on a quoting process or at least a rough planning process. But while almost all plants have some sort of expectation, the big question is whether or not they measure against this expectation. It almost goes without saying that reaching a goal is more feasible when everyone knows what it is; this extends to understanding why a goal was or was not achieved.

If you hand someone a work order to complete without associating a time with it, you are basically saying it will take whatever time it takes. This can be compared to having work done on your house or car without getting an estimate of how much the work will cost and how long it will take to do. In conducting your business, you probably estimate a time for a job when you established the price, so why not use that time as an expectation on the shop floor and learn from it? This does not mean gathering data weekly or monthly and lumping it into a report; instead, it means measuring small tasks in real time and addressing problems as they arise, when you are still able to alter the outcome and affect productivity.

If your scheduling is based only on the sequence of which job comes next, you do not have a schedule. You have only a sequence of priorities. You cannot understand schedule adherence or load and balance your processes efficiently. Once you adopt these tools, you can decide to use the additional time you have saved by either selling the increased capacity or reducing your labor cost.

Takt Time

Before proceeding with this discussion of the association of time with all work, let's clarify some terminology and discuss which method of managing production (takt time or day-by-hour) is appropriate for which type of production.

If you have processes dedicated to certain products, or a process that produces various dedicated part numbers that have reasonable forecasts, calculate a takt time (or various takt times, in the case of various part numbers) and manage your process based on customer requirements. (Having enough production volume that machines can be dedicated to certain part numbers is typical of high-volume production.)

$$\text{Pure takt time} = \frac{\text{time available (period)}}{\text{customer demand (period)}} = \frac{7.5 \text{ hours/day}}{15 \text{ units/day}} = 0.5 \text{ hours/unit}$$

Note: The time period for the numerator and denominator must be the same.

Takt is a word of German origin meaning pace or drumbeat. Simply put, *takt time* is the average rate at which a customer consumes one part; therefore, the part should also be produced at this rate. It is the time you manage by and decides whether you are ahead or behind. It should be used to balance previous and forthcoming processes. If you are building various parts on the same machine, calculate a separate takt time for each part based on how much of the machine's time is available for that particular part. This is called a pure calculation, because you are not taking into account any problems the process might experience. To take those problems into account, use overall equipment effectiveness (OEE; discussed in detail in chapter 10) or the uptime, and calculate the actual takt time.

Actual takt time = pure takt time × OEE (overall equipment effectiveness, or uptime) = 0.5 hours/unit × 75% OEE = 0.375 hours/unit

When you take into effect the OEE (or uptime), you have less available time within which to produce the part, as shown with the resultant 0.375 hours. This is the time you plan with and compare with your *cycle times* (that is, the time required to perform the work, usually per operator).

Cycle time is usually based on a time study of the work involved, and this number is compared to the actual takt time. The result is usually displayed in an operator balance wall, as discussed in chapter 9.

If instead you have a shared process (not dedicated to any particular products) or you build to order (without a forecast) as happens in most low-volume and job-shop plants, you need to associate a time with the work, and then manage the process with a day-by-hour board, as presented in chapter 4. In this case, you will *not* use takt time, because it is difficult to apply (it would require daily calculations, and it is too time-consuming to determine the time available for each part number on a frequent basis and customer demand is only known on an order-by-order basis).

Estimating Sheet

Another benefit of associating a time with your work is that it enables a better understanding of the accuracy of the estimates. You can use this feedback to improve your estimating process, and this helps you become better at costing/pricing products and acquiring a better understanding of your gross margin. A personal example easily illustrates this concept.

Two months after I opened my own business, my estimator suddenly quit and I found myself filling the position. I had little experience, so I set up a standard estimation sheet that would allow me to account for all possible costs methodically. Moreover, I had my operators track their time directly on the estimating sheet for each work operation and note any problems. I reviewed these sheets every Friday, and learned a lot. Naturally, I made mistakes, but the sheets helped me understand exactly what I had done wrong, so that I did not make the same mistake twice. One benefit to using an estimating sheet was that the operators soon became aware of the importance of trying to complete every job within the allotted time and what this implied for the longevity of the business, as they understood we were only paid based on the estimated time, not on a potentially longer time.

Figure 3-1 shows an estimating sheet, which includes columns for estimated setup time, estimated run time, actual time, and problems. By multiplying the run time per piece (for a particular operation) by the quantity of pieces in the order, then adding the setup time, you can plan how long the total operation will take and manage accordingly (for example, in operation 1 of Figure 3-1, 2 minutes $\times$ 30 pieces = 60 minutes). By adding the 0.33 hrs (20 minutes) of setup time, you know that the first operation should be complete in one hour, 20 minutes.

Part #: 877-29921-0 rev A   Qty: 30 pcs

Customer: ABC Inc.   Date: Jan 8, 2006

	Set up (hrs)	Run time (mins)	Actual time (completed by operator)	Problems encountered
Program	0.5	N/A		
Operation 1	0.33	2	1.5 hrs	broken drill
Operation 2	0.75	4		
Operation 3	1.25	9		
Operation 4				
Other				
Deburr	0	12		
Plating		$2 ea		
Stress Relieve	0	0		
Material	N/A			
Total time	2.83	27		
Total cost	$170	$29 ea		

Figure 3-1. An estimating and tracking sheet.

The operator can then directly fill in his or her actual time on the estimating sheet. Once this sheet is completed, you have accomplished two goals:

- You have increased productivity, because the operator is now conscious of the time he or she spends on the operation and works more diligently.

- The estimator learns how accurate he or she is and what problems were encountered.

If You Estimate Each Job

If you estimate each job, share the quoted time with your operators and have them track their time and problems against it. You'll need to know the following:

- Whether there were significant problems
- At which operation any problems occurred
- Whether it was a one-time occurrence
- Whether the problem could repeat itself in the future

You must have enough detail from the operator's description to decide the following:

- Whether it was a poor estimate
- Whether a problem is a repeating one
- Whether a problem was caused by the particular part or related to the machine or general process
- Whether a problem was caused by operator error
- The root cause of a problem (the conditions when it occurred; the specifics of what occurred)

Analyze this data in a simple way so that you can solve the most significant problems. The problems that are linked to a particular type of job and cannot be quickly resolved are indicators that you might need to add time (and, therefore, cost) on those types of jobs until a solution can be found. There is no sense in making a schedule and setting a price that you know cannot be maintained. (It is better to estimate and manage with realistic times and, if necessary, have a variable/adjustable labor rate based on the particular customer or market.)

Asking operators to time jobs is usually not time-consuming and can be simplified using an easy format. If setup time is involved, ask the operator to let you know the total time for getting the first part off the machine/process (total time for the first part = setup time + run time + any quality checking time), and then the run time of at least one additional part that did not encounter problems. You can then subtract this run time from the first combined time, and you have the setup time. This formula should be completed for each operation and is illustrated in Figure 3-2.

Figure 3-2. Separating setup and run time.

If Time Study Is Required, Visually Record the Processes

Observing and taking time measurements simultaneously is a difficult task and often requires observing the same operation more then once. This can be a challenge for low-volume operations, where you might only produce one piece on an infrequent basis. A recommended approach is to record the operation (on video, DVD, or digital media), which presents many options: rewind, slow motion, pause, and the ability to use an on-screen timer instead of a stopwatch. If you use a digital camcorder (which will not display an on-screen timer in minutes and seconds), you can use software like Power DVD to review the recording and view the minutes and seconds while watching.

It is important to film the hands doing the work and not get the operator's backside. If the operator has a significant distance to walk, also film the feet, so that you can evaluate the nature of the walking distance and can work on improvements if necessary.

Some operators will shy away from being videotaped, so don't force the issue. Once you have one or two jobs filmed and the operators are allowed to view the recording(s), they will understand that the focus is on the operation rather than on the individual performing the operation and will recognize the value of the filming process and what it implies for future work. An additional benefit is that the videotape can be used to train other operators on the process.

If There Are No Standard Times for Each Specific Part Number

In many low-volume plants, there may be thousands of part numbers, and it is nearly impossible to develop production times for every part number. If this is the situation in your plant and you do not have accurate data available, the simplest thing to do is group similar parts into families and use the same times for product families with similar process steps. A logical way to sort and group parts is by size and complexity. This is easiest to do in a spreadsheet format, especially if a part number or description helps to identify the size of each part and its complexity.

The plant presented in Figure 3-3 has two processes, machining and assembly. Because a part that may require complex machining may be easy to assemble, we need two different groupings of time.

In the system this plant has developed for part numbers the first three digits indicate the product type (220 = manual and 240 = electrical). This is important because it affects the process time. The last letter in the part indicates the material (S = steel and L = stainless steel), which also affects the machining time. The machine time is affected by:

- The diameter

- Whether the part calls for tight tolerance
- Whether small cushioning holes have to be drilled
- Whether it has a machined cavity for an air bleed

Part Number	Description	tight tolerance	cushion port	air bleed	Quantity of Assy components on Bill of Material	Assigned Group number for machine time	Assigned Group number for assembly time
220-113-15S	15mm proportion		X	X	20	B	B
220-148-28S	28mm 2 stage				20	A	B
220-186-55S	55mm proportion			X	20	B	C
220-129-15L	15mm high press 1 stage	X	X	X	32	C	C
220-154-36L	36mm proportion			X	28	D	B
240-132-20S	20mm electronic 2 stage		X		14	A	A

Figure 3-3. Grouping similar parts into product families.

This type of specific knowledge is provided by the manufacturing team, and they can develop the timetable as shown in Figure 3-4. Assembly time (also shown in Figure 3-4) is affected by:

- The size of the part
- The number of components
- Whether the part is electronic or mechanical

Times for machining (by group type)	Times for assembly (by group type)
A = 20 min.	A = 11 min.
B = 24 min.	B = 19 min.
C = 29 min.	C = 27 min.
D = 34 min.	

Figure 3-4. Machining and assembly times for the product families.

Note that the "15 mm proportion" valve (listed in Figure 3-3) is in machining group B, because it has a small diameter, does not have tight tolerance, and has a cushion port and air bleed that require machining. Grouping products into families with similar work content, and then developing an average working time for that family is a good method if you have many part numbers with similar characteristics.

If You Have Repetitive Parts with Standard Costs

In a low-volume business, you may sell your parts for a standard cost plus some type of margin. These standard costs are usually based on standard times; therefore, you have a basis on which to make a schedule. Compare each operation against its standard time. If you find that actual times (that is, when the operator does not encounter significant problems) vary by more than +/– 15 percent, change the standard time. Always base any changes on more than one timing, however, and the more data the better. But do not wait too long to begin adjusting times. Times taken that are within 15 percent of the standard should be acceptable unless you have a small enough number of parts and enough confidence and repeatability in your manufacturing to start adjusting even those times. The obvious cautions are that there can be many reasons for the variations; normally, accuracy within +/– 15 percent is acceptable and tends to balance itself out.

If your pricing policy has been to take your costs and add a margin to determine the customer price, and then you begin to learn that the time it takes you to perform an operation is different, you now have a different cost, which means you will have a different customer price. Of course, if the actual time for an operation is longer or shorter than the time estimated, you might want to consider raising or lowering the price accordingly, unless you feel that the current price is tolerated by your customers and acceptable to you. If you decide not to change your pricing to accommodate differences in estimated time and actual time, use one of the following options:

- Use a variable labor rate (higher or lower) to absorb the difference:

$$\text{Variable labor rate} = \frac{\text{sales price} - (\text{profit} + \text{all costs other than labor})}{\text{actual hours}}$$

- Use a variable profit margin to absorb the difference:

$$\text{Profit} = \text{sales} - \text{all costs (including actual labor hours} \times \text{a standard labor rate)}$$

The important thing is to schedule and base productivity on actual time. For this reason, it is important to have the actual time in your system or records so you can plan accurately and understand your actual margins and estimating ability.

If You're Guessing

Some plants simply plug in their experience and make their best guess at an hourly target, but this can be dangerous if you are not accurate. If you set the target too low, you can motivate some operators to underperform; if the target is set too high, the suggested rate will be viewed as unrealistic and will be ignored. Your best bet is to set the target slightly higher than is currently achievable, and then work on improvements to reach it. At the same time, let workers know that the working time should continue to decrease as more improvements are implemented.

Whatever method you use to associate a time with the work, you need to visually track your actual time against the estimated time to obtain productivity improvements. Effective use of day-by-hour charts to accomplish this is presented in chapter 4.

Summary of Key Points

- Associating a time with each job (on an operation-by-operation basis) is critical to scheduling, productivity, product costing, and accurate estimating.

- Not setting a target time for when tasks should be completed is like writing a blank check.

- There are different methods to arrive at a time for each operation:
    - Estimates
    - Operator feedback
    - Analyzing and adjusting standard costing
    - Time study
    - Grouping similar parts into product families and using an average time

- Once a time is associated with each task, you must measure against this to realize a productivity increase.

4

Utilizing Day-by-Hour and FIFO Boards

This chapter augments the material discussed in chapter 3; it assumes you have a method to quantify how long a task should take and focuses on methods to set expectations, monitor them, and document any problems. *Monitoring* refers to regular observation and recording of activities. Many plants, simply by setting expectations and by monitoring work methods, see productivity improve by 10 percent to 15 percent. Much of this improvement comes from having people at their workstations on time, producing when they should, and working on the correct priorities.

When monitoring, you learn the accuracy of your estimating and can adjust it as necessary, not only to manage production, but also to improve your product costing (see chapter 3). Start by monitoring production areas, but recognize that monitoring can also improve performance in other departments. The chart in Figure 4-1 (presented in color on page 20) illustrates this point by showing the progress and a goal for configuring orders in an engineering department. To set the goal, the department had to determine how many systems could be configured in one day; there is now a standard time for this, and the department staff can track it. Although hourly measurements are ideal in a production area, daily measurement is generally reasonable in an office environment.

Keep in mind that for every process you monitor for productivity, you will need to provide a place to describe the reasons or problems that lead to targets not being met. If the management team is not ready to address some of those problems, the operators being monitored will become discouraged and this will have an adverse affect on productivity. For this reason, it is best to begin only with those processes you can support with problem-solving resources (for example, focus only on the bottleneck that is causing an entire process to slow down).

The Role of Production Control

In a lean environment, the production control department plays an absolutely vital role and is responsible for very detailed planning. This includes capacity planning down to a machine or process level. Getting all the right parts to the right point on time is probably one of your biggest issues and if production control does not understand true lead times, you have little chance of success. Since lead time varies in high mix, and traditional MRP systems assume a constant lead time, you need another method that shows when and where lead times are varying so you can react; day-by-hour boards can help.

Production control cannot simply tell sales that the capacity is "about $100,000/month" and provide production with "a list of priorities." Instead, production control must make a daily or hourly plan for each process, as compared with process capabilities. This planning requires understanding the work content of each job and then scheduling that job to accommodate machine capability and lead time. Naturally, this information is balanced against all other lead times in the flow, along with the customer's requirements. The planning also includes detailed feedback to sales about which processes (and, therefore, which products) are at capacity for a given period and which still have additional capacity that can be sold. Production control must take an active role in completing the day-by-hour boards (discussed in the following section) and ensure that materials are available.

Since installing "pull" systems throughout the entire flow are not possible in high mix because you almost never build to a finished goods inventory, you will push (based on lead time and other factors) at the first operation and then flow through the remaining processes.

Note: In some cases, where a machine performs the first operation for some parts and a later operation (second, third, or fourth step) for other parts, production control will be able to schedule only the parts beginning on this machine, the others will arrive randomly and be scheduled using a FIFO board, which is discussed later in this chapter. Sometimes, day-by-hour and FIFO boards are used simultaneously.

Day-by-Hour Boards

Day-by-hour boards are best utilized with shared processes where you are usually working without a solid forecast. A quick look at a day-by-hour board should enable the following:

- Capacity planning at a glance
- An ability to prioritize
- An ability to visualize the current status versus the plan
- Indicates where you currently have an imbalance of work
- A way to encourage operators to list problems that cause delays

General Benefits from Day-by-Hour Boards

The greatest immediate benefit to come from day-by-hour boards is productivity improvement from time lost because of random starting and ending times of operating the machine or process, workers returning from breaks at a leisurely pace or talking to other operators, and so on. As the supervisor's awareness of problems and delays increases, he or she can become more proactive in reducing problems as they occur and meeting the schedule. Other benefits include the following:

- Operators will become more proactive about pointing out problems that do not allow them to complete a job in the allotted time (they can now speak with "data").
- It becomes easier to measure productivity improvements.
- It becomes easier to understand accuracy of estimates or standard times.
- Operators are encouraged to achieve or exceed the goal.
- Managers can see how close they are to the planned or estimated times (which equate to costs and, therefore, profits).

For some it helps to continuously understand where they are in relation to the plan and try to pull orders through on time, instead of managing by the "end-of-month crunch" in order to profitably close the books.

Types of Day-by-Hour Boards

For visualizing and tracking productivity in production, there are four general types of day-by-hour boards. These are shown in Figure 4-2 and discussed in the following sections. Remember to target your first boards at the bottleneck operations.

	Type of Board	Description of process	Dedicated process for certain parts
I.	Day-by-hour board - Type A	Intermediate or final process, process times normally less than 1 hour, rare for same part to repeat	No
II.	Day-by-hour board - Type B	Intermediate or final process, process times normally greater than 1 hour, rare for same part to repeat	No
III.	Combined kanban & work order board (also used to help level spikes in demand)	Intermediate or final process, process times normally less than 1 hour, some higher volume parts repeat more regularly & other low volumes repeat infrequently or never (*this board is used where some parts can have a small inventory build up—this will help level demand with capacity*)	Yes
IV.	Progress cards	For a systems manufacturer, process times are significantly greater than 1 hour and in some cases measured in days	Yes

Figure 4-2. Four types of day-by-hour boards.

Day-by-Hour Board, Type A

Use the type-A board when a part or unit takes less then one hour to complete.

One way to set targets is to schedule a process according to what should be completed each hour. Figures 4-3 and 4-4 present two examples of type-A boards. Figure 4-3 is an interdepartmental board for a honing machine in a machine shop. As machining centers finish parts, they are lined up for honing. The planner comes at set intervals and schedules and prioritizes parts; the parts are grouped into hourly blocks (hence the name day-by-hour) so the operator can record (every hour) the quantity completed and any problems encountered. (The planner needs to know what is a reasonable hourly target for each type of part.) The work order may be large and may require many hours of work, but only hourly quantities should be posted on the board. It is helpful to install an electronic sound signal that reminds the operator to record his or her results every hour. If you use an erasable board for this purpose, ask workers to document problems on paper as this facilitates analyzing and saving this data.

Figure 4-3. Day-by-hour board, type A: hourly targets for a honing machine.

Figure 4-4 shows a board that can be generated manually or electronically. From the shift's starting time, each order is scheduled according to the presumed amount of time it should take. Some managers find it useful to build a 10 percent to 15 percent allowance into this anticipated timeframe. This day-by-hour board is a simple visual schedule that is adjusted with feedback from the operator; it keeps operators conscious of the time being utilized and apprises management of any problems.

Date: _1/24/2006_

Machine: _Haas #6_

Order number	Part number	Due date	Quantity Ordered	Quantity planned	Priority	Planned time (min)	Planned start time	Planned finish time	Actual quantity completed	Actual finish time	Problems/Comments
398221	714-2230	2/27/2006	5	5	A	0:24	10:15	10:39			
456883	714-2290	2/27/2006	4	4	A	0:33	10:39	11:12			
561001	715-0987	2/29/2006	8	8		0:39	11:12	11:52			
931123	714-3311	2/30/2006	7	7		0:37	11:52	13:11			
87331	716-9012	2/30/2006	9	9	B	0:34	13:11	13:46			
453321	714-8002	3/1/2006	1	1		0:17	13:46	14:03			
						0:00					
						0:00					

Figure 4-4. Another day-by-hour board, type A: specific start and stop times for orders.

Day-by-Hour Board, Type B

Use this type of board when one part takes more than one hour to produce. Essentially, the board separates out all the steps necessary to complete the part and allows you to plan which steps can be completed within the hour. Figure 4-5 shows the number of valve sections scheduled per hour. Because a valve is a combination of valve sections, a complete part can consist of two to ten sections. Each valve can take anywhere from twenty minutes to two hours to complete though it is known the operators can assemble four to seven sections per hour, depending on the complexity of the section type. Therefore, it is easiest to schedule a number of sections per hour, as displayed in the "Goal" column. Take into account how much time and effort goes into assembling particular sections and the number of operators available for this purpose (in the case illustrated in Figure 4-5, there are five operators). Once these factors are determined, the planner can adjust the goal accordingly (e.g., from four to six value sections per hour), instead of trying to schedule completed valves, which can take significantly longer than one hour.

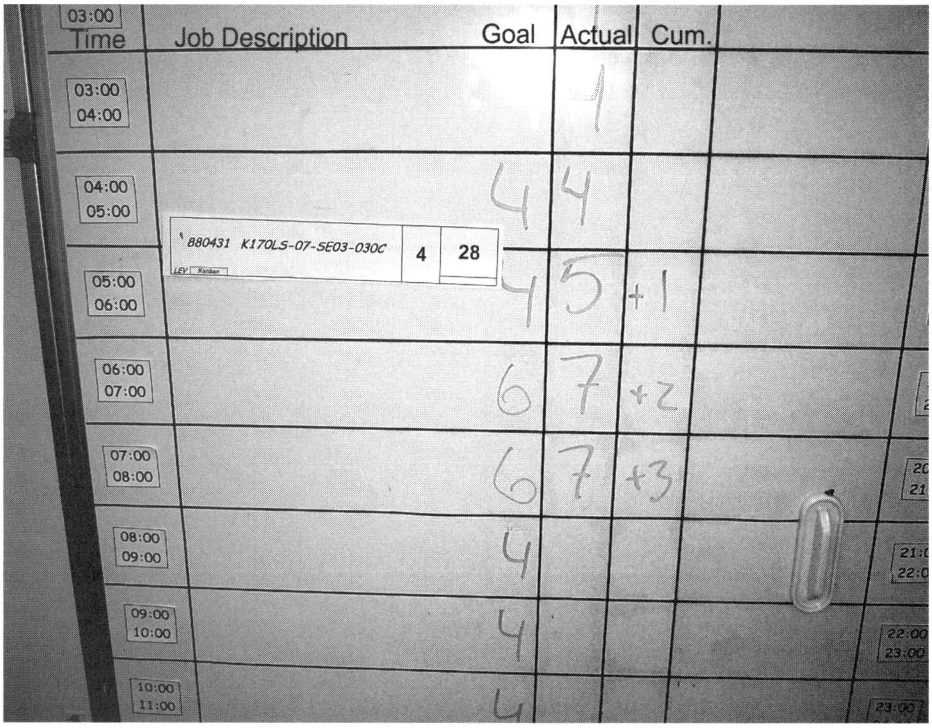

Figure 4-5. Type-B day-by-hour board: complete part separated by valve sections.

The *scheduling box* shown in Figure 4-6 can be used for either type-A or type-B boards (jobs shorter or longer than one hour). It is best used when all jobs are printed on work orders and all work orders note work time. A *work order* is usually a piece of paper produced for each job that authorizes production to make a specific part. It contains information such as the customer's name, due date, quantity, process steps, and time to complete each step. To use the scheduling box, simply take your work orders for the next one or two shifts (using a maximum of 24 hours) and match them to the operator (or process) that should perform the work, according to the necessary time to complete each order.

Scheduling Box

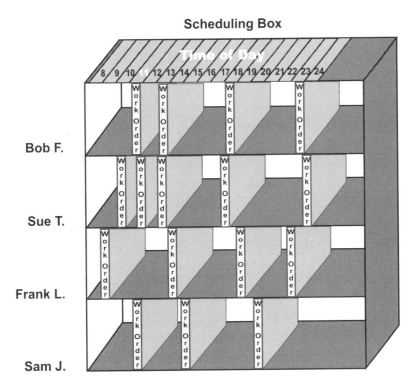

Figure 4-6. Scheduling box.

Because each work order specifies the time necessary to complete the job, you know when you can schedule the next work order. This system also requires operators working in a common area to work on the job you specify and allows you to see whether operators are ahead of or behind schedule. For example, as Figure 4-6 shows, Sue T. was to start working on a new work order at 10:00 A.M. Assume it is now 11:00 A.M. and you can easily see that she is at least one hour behind as she has not begun the work order (orders are removed from the box when the operator starts working on them).

Combination Kanban and Work-Order Board

Kanban is a signaling system based on consumption that is set up to replace what the customer consumes; it is a type of pull system. A *combination kanban and work-order board* is often used in the following circumstances:

- You have some parts that are repeatedly ordered and others that are low volume and are ordered periodically or just-in-time.

- You have a changeover time involved.
- Your customer order quantity and lead time vary from order to order.

This also assumes that both the repeaters and nonrepeaters are manufactured in the same process or machine. The board can be utilized for parts taking less than or more than one hour to produce. *Note:* Many companies need work orders to authorize production and to use as a tracking tool for materials, costs, and so on. When most kanban systems are installed, a method to link a work order with a kanban card is put in place. Some companies preprint a few work orders for each kanban part with the same quantity shown on the kanban card, and then the operator uses the available work order to authorize and track the production.

Take, for example, a plastic injection molding machine, at which you manufacture parts according to customers' specifications. You probably have some parts that receive repeat orders—your *high runners*. By studying the size and regularity of those orders and using any forecasts from the customer, you can plan to manufacture some of those parts to a small, predetermined inventory level without having a solid order (that is, a pull system triggered by kanban) without much risk of creating obsolete inventory.

The lean way to do this is to put those part numbers on a kanban (which means you determine a minimum and maximum level you would like to maintain in stock and replace parts only when the minimum is reached). This "extra" inventory may cause you to wonder, "Is this really lean?" This question often arises, but instead of being hidden inventory that is ordered by a computer program, it is openly displayed on the kanban board. This visibility ensures it is regularly challenged by everyone who has some grasp of lean principles. Note, however, that the inventory is there because you cannot eliminate changeover time or level your various customers' demands with your capacity. For this reason, you can build some low-risk inventory during slow periods, which means that during busy periods, you will already have some work complete and in stock, ready to ship, and this will help you balance peak workloads and increase on-time delivery as shown in Figure 4-7. If you select the right parts for kanban and calculate the level correctly, you will not carry much inventory, and the flexibility in balancing your workload and increasing your on-time delivery will offset the small risk and inventory costs.

The trick is to make sure this level is reviewed frequently for changes in forecasts, reductions in setup times, and changes in other parameters. Moreover, because keeping some stock will reduce lead time, you may find the customer is willing to share the risk and purchase this small amount of inventory in the event that the part becomes obsolete at some future time.

Caution: If you believe quality problems will be an issue with this inventory, you are probably *not* in a position to consider this approach.

There are some simple ways to calculate how many parts (or kanbans) you want for a specific part number (this is discussed in more detail in chapter 8). Low-volume parts that do not have repeating orders (i.e., "built to order") normally are not setup as a kanban part and are instead managed by a work order. Combine both the repeating (kanban parts) and nonrepeating parts (work order parts) on the same board, so that you can see all incoming work in a given process, and then schedule it in one place, this is called a "combination kanban work order board." The advantages to using a combined board are numerous.

- Kanban parts are simple to plan (and do not require MRP or considerable time from production control).

- The inventory status of the parts is always known by everyone (the board is a reverse image of your inventory; a card on the board means an empty space in your inventory).

- Kanban parts help smooth customer demand (see Figure 4-7).

- It is easy to prioritize kanbans and work orders.

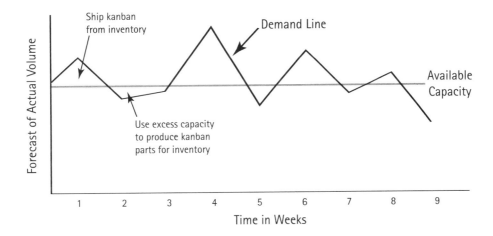

Figure 4-7. Demand versus capacity for a typical process.

In Figure 4-7, during the high demand in week 1, you can ship some kanban parts and lower your workload, bringing it in line with capacity. During the low demand in week 2, you can build kanban parts and replenish the inventory, balancing your operations with capacity. Overall, you can balance your capacity with the changes in customer demand, assuming you have a sufficient number of parts on kanban.

Note: Some of this workload fluctuation from week to week can also be caused by customers infrequently ordering large quantities, instead of placing frequent orders for smaller quantities. This phenomenon is frequently caused by the pricing policy, the cost to process an order, the perceived extra cost to ship (although most shipping costs are based on weight), the parameters used when your customer set up their MRP system, and so on. Review the reasons behind this with your customers; they may be willing to consider changing their order patterns, especially if they recognize that they seldom consume a large quantity at one time and the bulk of a large order just sits in their inventory. If you can get them to change their ordering policies, you can also balance your capacity.

Figure 4-8 (reproduced in color on page 20) shows a combined kanban and work-order board that includes day-by-hour. This example is used when you build various low-volume products in one process according to customer orders, but some of those low volumes are regularly repeating parts that are set up on kanban with a small amount of inventory. This helps to smooth cyclical workloads as you can use slow order periods to refill kanbans, a small risk if well planned (see chapter 8), and during busy periods, you already have these regular parts on the shelf.

This type of board can be divided into three sections:

Section A, the kanban status is shown on the top part of the board. Because there was significant volume on fifteen part numbers, these were set up as kanban parts. A kanban level was calculated for each part, and a hook was put on the board to represent each card. The kanban card stays with the parts while they are in inventory, but as soon as parts ship to the customer, the card is returned to the board (see Figure 4-9). Therefore, a card on the board signals an empty space in the inventory, while an empty hook means you have the completed parts stored in inventory. The hooks are color coded green, yellow, and red. As the inventory is shipped, the cards return and fill the green hooks first, but as you continue to ship, you start to fill the yellow hooks, and finally, as you use the last of your inventory, you fill the red hooks (see Figure 4-10 on page 21).

The kanban cards need to include the manufacturing time so you are able to develop a schedule on the day-by-hour section of this board. Figure 4-10 illustrates this, with 1.8 hours for each kanban card to produce the twelve pieces.

This type of board ensures that everyone is aware of inventory status and can prioritize accordingly. Moreover, it promotes a level of team involvement and cooperation that is seldom possible when inventory calculations are performed by a computer. Everyone understands how many parts are in inventory and why the inventory is necessary, and everyone can participate in monitoring and adjusting inventory levels as needed.

In **Section B**, on the bottom part of the board, the work orders are continuously placed in two baskets. As this is a short lead-time business, orders are grouped by what must be manufactured today and what is due the following week. The work orders must also include a standard completion time (usually in minutes) so they can be scheduled just like the kanban cards.

Kanban card is removed and returned to the board after using the first or last part in the box.

Figure 4-9. Kanban card stays with box until parts are consumed.

The actual scheduling is done in **Section C**. Once a day (at the same hour each day), the planner and team leader come together and prioritize work orders and kanbans on the hooks in the center section of the board (each hook represents one-half hour). They schedule for the next twenty-four-hour period, but not longer, because a lot can go wrong in one day. The outcome of their meeting becomes not only the schedule but also the production tracking board. If it is 11:30 in the morning and work orders that were scheduled for 9:30 are still hanging on the board, the board indicates that production is about two hours behind. On these boards, you also want to provide a place for the operator to note problems and show a tracking sheet of which past problems are currently being resolved. (An example of this type of action plan is shown on the team boards in chapter 1.)

Many variations of this board can be adapted to your type of business. Make sure the board is set up to be flexible: Because customer demands continuously change, kanban levels must be continuously readjusted. Simply stated, you are trying to visualize the incoming work and determine a schedule based on priorities.

Figure 4-8 (page 20) shows kanban parts that, when grouped in small batch quantities on each card, take over one hour to manufacture. Each hook represents one-half hour, so you can see that a card is scheduled every three to four hooks on the day-by-hour timeline.

Deciding who schedules the production into hourly increments usually depends on the size and support functions in the organization. It also may depend on how often new work orders and kanbans are posted on the board and the lead time promised to the customer. Normally, if the lead time is short (one day or less), it is best to have the team leader or operator continuously reprioritize the board. Rules should clearly define how priorities are established, and management should monitor the process and support the operator by providing additional help or allowing overtime as required to meet deadlines.

If production control is responsible for planning, the team leader should still have input. Normally, scheduling is done once a day, at approximately the same time each day. For example, some plants find it practical to create a schedule that runs from 10:00 A.M. of one day to 10:00 A.M. the next day. This allows the planner to have some time to review incoming work in the morning, determine priorities based on customer requests, determine the availability of materials, and the availability of labor. Some plants choose to create schedules that are based on when they receive information from customers. Job shops where this approach is preferred invariably require frequent updates to the schedule.

If you have lots of final part numbers with only small variations among them, kanbans can be set up for incomplete assemblies that require only a small step to finalize them to a specific part number—in other words, assemble as far as possible until the large variation is introduced, but leave one or two small assembly steps (where a lot of variation is introduced) until the order is placed. This can significantly reduce peak workloads with low risk. When the order is received, the kanban part is pulled from the shelf (which sends the card back to the board, essentially ordering another one), and the final assembly work is quickly done. This keeps the lead time short, and variation in workload from the customer is minimized.

Progress Cards

If you build systems that contain more than one process and take days or weeks to build, you can utilize *progress* cards. One card can represent each final assembly, and this card should show all the processes required to complete the assembly in the sequenced order of build. Sometimes, the card can also represent the approximate time for each step. See Figure 4-11, in which the operator shades/colors each process step as he or she completes it; this way, everyone understands the current status.

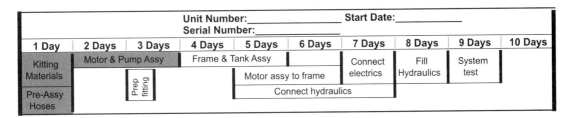

Figure 4-11. Progress card.

Having operators shade areas as they finish each operation allows you to use the progress cards for planning and tracking. These cards can be put on a board (see Figure 4-12) to show the schedule and whether you are on time or behind. It is a good idea to use cards with magnetic backing and lamination so erasable markers can be used.

As Figure 4-12 illustrates, a card is started for each system/unit, which is scheduled on the board by the planner. The operators shade the areas as they finish the respective tasks. In this example, a gray strip is moved across to today's date (in this example, May 17). You can see immediately that the first unit is ahead and the next three are late to varying degrees. For companies building complex parts, daily planning like this is likely too difficult to implement as a first step. If this is the case in your company, you can begin by grouping the progress cards by week to reflect when you expect the unit to be complete, upgrading to daily planning once everyone is more comfortable and more experienced with the approach. In either case, include a board to list the problems and track their resolution.

The progress card board in Figure 4-13 shows systems that take four to five days to build. The process steps (for example, kit parts, paint, assemble motor/tank, assemble hoses, test) are listed in sequential order, although in some cases, processes can happen simultaneously. The cards are frequently attached with magnets or Velcro. The cards can be reprioritized, depending on changing customer requirements or production delays. Each card represents a complete unit and can be placed in an overall timeline. Note that, in Figure 4-13, the progress cards are not linked to a timeline; instead, they are placed in order of priority and grouped by the week in which they are due. The first step is just to use a card for each system to understand what is complete or incomplete, and line them up into an order of priorities. Later, the plant can introduce the timeline and demonstrate whether orders are on time or late.

Hydraulic Pump Cell - Day by hour

| 8-May | 9-May | 10-May | 11-May | 12-May | 15-May | 16-May | 17-May | 18-May | 19-May | 22-May | 23-May | 24-May | 25-May | 26-May | 29-May | 30-May | 31-May | 1-Jun | 2-Jun |

Start Date: 5 May
Unit Number: 124887E
Serial Number: 93356EF2

1 Day	2 Days	3 Days	4 Days	5 Days	6 Days	7 Days	8 Days	9 Days	10 Days
Kitting Material	Motor & Pump Assy	Prep fittings	Frame & Tank Assy	Motor assy to frame	Connect hydraulics	Connect electrics	Fill Hydraulics	System test	
Pre-Assy Hoses									

Start Date: 10 May
Unit Number: 277188TY
Serial Number: 93355RD2

1 Day	2 Days	3 Days	4 Days	5 Days	6 Days	7 Days	8 Days	9 Days	10 Days
Kitting Materials	Motor & Pump Assy	Prep fittings	Frame & Tank Assy	Motor Assy to Frame	Connect hydraulics	Connect electrics	Fill Hydraulics	System test	
Pre-Assy Hoses									

Start Date: 12 May
Unit Number: 458830PP
Serial Number: 93357RR2

1 Day	2 Days	3 Days	4 Days	5 Days	6 Days	7 Days	8 Days	9 Days	10 Days
Kitting Materials	Motor & Pump Assy	Prep fittings	Frame & Tank Assy	Motor assy to frame	Connect hydraulics	Connect electrics	Fill Hydraulics	System test	
Pre-Assy Hoses									

Start Date: 17 May
Unit Number:433991US
Serial Number: 76550OP

1 Day	2 Days	3 Days	4 Days	5 Days	6 Days	7 Days	8 Days	9 Days	10 Days
Kitting Materials	Motor & Pump Assy	Prep fittings	Frame & Tank Assy	Motor assy to frame	Connect hydraulics	Connect electrics	Fill Hydraulics	System test	
Pre-Assy Hoses									

Figure 4-12. Progress card board.

58

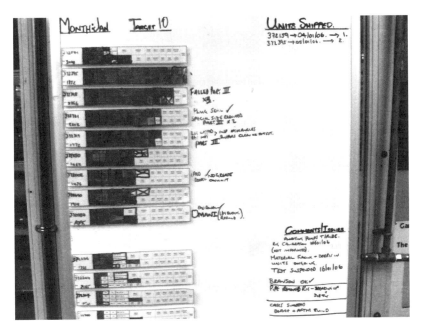

Figure 4-13. Progress card board in use.

First-In, First-Out Boards

First-in, first-out (FIFO) boards are used where work orders route jobs through various processes (depending on their requirements), making it difficult to know when a particular job will arrive at a particular process and, therefore, difficult to balance the workload at each process. This type of board helps you understand how much work is waiting at various processes so that you can rebalance manpower accordingly. An example is a machine shop in which various parts are routed to various machines. Part A might go to be premachined on the small mill and finish machined on the large mill, but part B might go to the lathe, then to the large mill, and so on. This type of board is best utilized in the following situations:

- When work is randomly placed in front of the process, and the sequence in which it arrives determines the processing order.

- When work orders route jobs through various processes (depending on their requirements), making it difficult to balance the workload at each process.

- In combination with a day-by-hour board, when a machine is the first process for some part numbers and is a second, third, or fourth process step for other part numbers. (In this case, the overall priority between the two boards is set by the team leader or planner on a timeline.)

In Figure 4-14, each gray circle is a magnet that can easily be moved, and each magnet represents 0.5 hours of work. The "work waiting" row shows there is 7.5 hours of work lined up in front of the process. The "work in progress" row tells you that the operator is currently processing a job that will take a total of two hours. The "work completed during current shift" shows that three hours of work has already been completed on this shift. An explanation of how the board functions is presented below the figure.

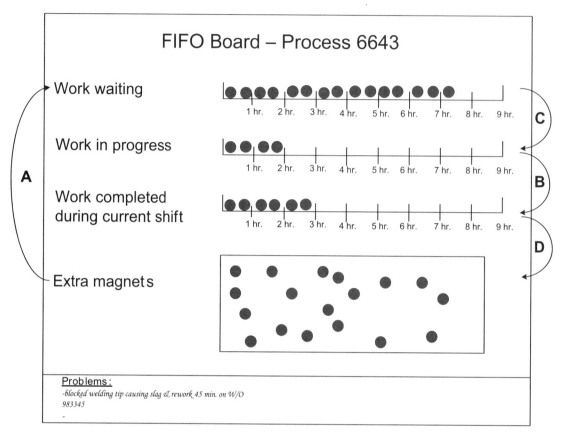

Figure 4-14. FIFO board.

- Reference A in Figure 4-14: Whoever delivers the work to this process should move the correct quantity of magnets from the "extra magnets" box to the "work waiting" line. The hours needed to complete this operation (process #6643) should be listed on the work order, which usually travels with the job. The overall size of the "work waiting" area should be based on the planned lead times and cycle times.

- Reference B in Figure 4-14: When the operator begins on a new job, he first moves the magnets from "work in progress" to "work completed during current shift" for the job he just finished. He or she should note any major problems discovered at the bottom of the board.

- Reference C in Figure 4-14: The operator then moves the correct quantity of magnets from "work waiting" to "work in progress" for the job he is about to begin.

- Reference D in Figure 4-14: Usually, the team leader or supervisor clears all the magnets from the "work completed during current shift" section and moves them to the "extra magnets" box at the end of the shift. This allows the team leader or supervisor to see how many hours of work were finished (this can be recorded/tracked to look for trends).

Joining the Combined Kanban and Work-Order Board and the FIFO Board

When you have a machine that is the first process for some part numbers and a second, third, or fourth process for other part numbers, consider using a combined kanban and work-order board in conjunction with a FIFO board. When you combine these two boards, kanban cards and work orders are used to schedule all parts that begin their production sequence on this machine, and parts that have later operations at this same machine will be pushed into the FIFO lane when they are ready and are scheduled on the FIFO board. When parts are waiting in the FIFO area, the planner or team leader can use the yellow cards, shown in Figure 4-8 (reproduced in color on page 20) section C, both to schedule time on the combined kanban board and to work on parts waiting in FIFO. (Yellow cards are also sometimes used to schedule the machine for maintenance or other planned down times). Therefore, the priorities for kanban, work orders, and FIFO parts are all shown in one timeline in Figure 4-8 section C—you can see that this board contains the master schedule. If a kanban part must be routed to various other processes, the routing information can be provided on the back of the kanban card to let the operator know where to move the parts when the process is complete.

Recognizing the Danger of Putting Up Too Many Boards

The danger in putting up boards for all processes simultaneously is that they require considerable monitoring and support from management. Remember you are now asking operators to note every significant problem they encounter. This is a two-way street, so operators will expect management to work on resolving some of these problems. Although operators usually tell managers about problems, even without boards, this is normally done informally and without much data; managers are often lacking the necessary information (such as the magnitude of the problem) to prioritize problems. Managers can rely on experience to categorize and prioritize problems, but visual tools providing essential data (quantity of parts and time lost due to these problems) and some simple data analysis can make it easier to identify which problems are most costly.

Getting the Required Support

It should be made absolutely clear to the operators from the start that the support teams (production, engineering, quality) will not be able to work on all problems simultaneously and that these teams will be able to tackle only one or two of the most critical problems at any given time. During the process, communicate which problems are being worked on, by whom, and what the status is. Use a tracking sheet like the one shown in Figure 4-15; display it either on the day-by-hour board or the value stream board. This particular tracking sheet helps to promote compliance with the PDCA (plan, do, check, and act) cycle by having the red/yellow/green status updated weekly, so that everyone knows whether the improvement is on time according to the predetermined dates and is being "checked" for desired results.

Knowing Where to Begin with the First Boards

The best way to start is with one board on a relatively stable process that has some of the following characteristics (especially if it is a bottleneck process):

- Consistent quantity of work
- Stable process times
- Few problems
- Optimistic and proactive operators

Summary of Key Points

- Day-by-hour and FIFO boards drive productivity improvements by setting and measuring productivity expectations.
- Use either a day-by-hour board, FIFO board, or combination of both boards at each process. The type of board you use depends on the characteristics of the process.
- Day-by-hour or FIFO boards help show when you are behind (therefore not achieving the planned lead time), possibly in time to react and minimize the delay.
- Putting some repeating (higher volume) parts on kanban helps balance your capacity with fluctuations in customer demand.
- Even when manufacturing (or rebuilding) complex systems, you can adapt a form of day-by-hour; it is called a progress card.
- These boards should be put up sequentially (not all at once), starting with your most stable processes.
- A lot of management support is required to monitor and resolve problems communicated by these boards.
- Operators, team leaders, and production control need to be trained how to use the boards.

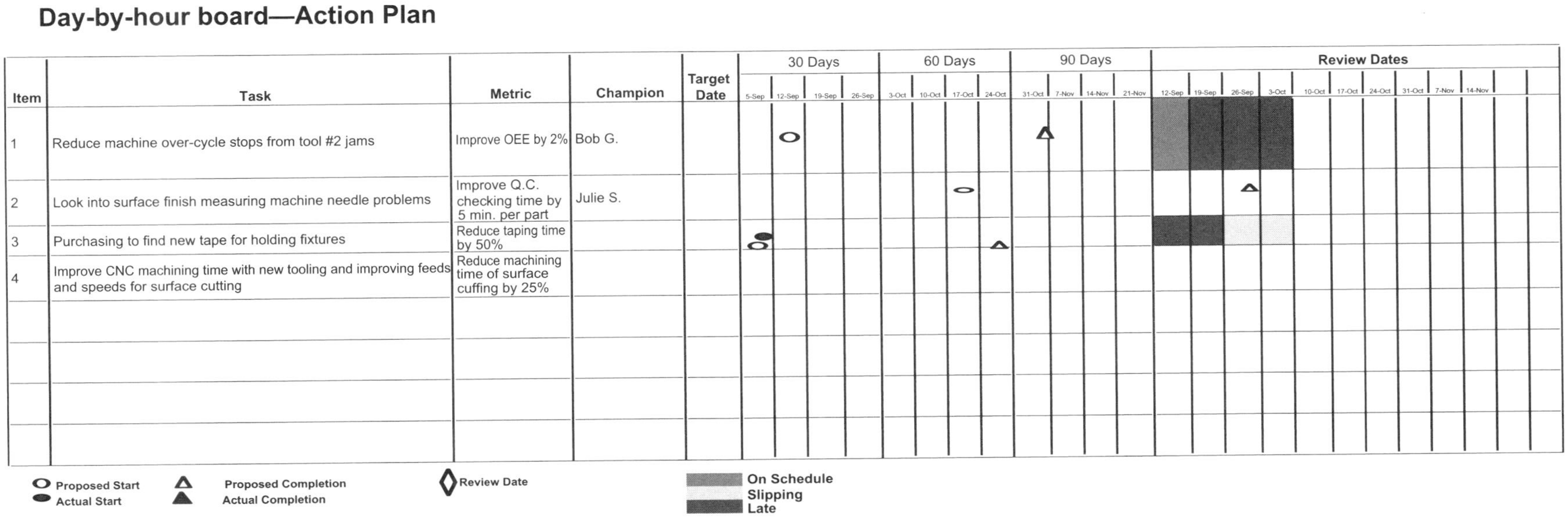
Day-by-hour board—Action Plan
Item
Task
Metric
Champion
Target Date
30 Days
60 Days
90 Days
Review Dates
5-Sep
12-Sep
19-Sep
26-Sep
3-Oct
10-Oct
17-Oct
24-Oct
31-Oct
7-Nov
14-Nov
21-Nov
12-Sep
19-Sep
26-Sep
3-Oct
10-Oct
17-Oct
24-Oct
31-Oct
7-Nov
14-Nov
1
Reduce machine over-cycle stops from tool #2 jams
Improve OEE by 2%
Bob G.
2
Look into surface finish measuring machine needle problems
Improve Q.C. checking time by 5 min. per part
Julie S.
3
Purchasing to find new tape for holding fixtures
Reduce taping time by 50%
4
Improve CNC machining time with new tooling and improving feeds and speeds for surface cutting
Reduce machining time of surface cuffing by 25%
Proposed Start
Actual Start
Proposed Completion
Actual Completion
Review Date
On Schedule
Slipping
Late

Figure 4-15. Example of tracking the improvements.

5

Making Improvements When You're Short of Capacity

When demand begins to exceed capacity, many companies move too quickly to outsource their excess demand or purchase new equipment. Often, these companies fail to consider the potential risks that these solutions bring with them. For example, when demand goes above a piece of equipment's current capacity, it usually increases only in small increments. But a new piece of equipment may double capacity and leave you with excess capacity and excess costs. Moreover, if outsourcing in your industry is quick and without significant start-up costs or delays, it may seem a logical solution, but be aware that it does not always produce expected and desired results. Before being swayed by the potential benefits of a new machine or outsourcing, review and implement the recommendations presented in this chapter. Keep in mind that most of the techniques in this chapter involve changing a working method, which means that, initially (while the operator is learning the new method), production will experience a temporarily negative effect. The learning curve is usually quick, however, and the long-term improvements can be very rewarding. Also keep in mind that most of these techniques should first be applied to your bottleneck processes.

Changeover Time Reduction: SMED

The *Single Minute Exchange of Dies (SMED) methodology* can be used to reduce the time for any type of changeover; it does not have to be a process that includes changing dies in a stamping or molding machine. The method was pioneered by Shigeo Shingo,[1] and the details can be found in many books. This

---

1. Shigeo Shingo, *A Revolution in Manufacturing: The SMED System.* Productivity Press: New York, 1985.

section does not provide a detailed overview but applies Shingo's ideas to a high-mix, low-volume environment.

Changeover time is the total time it takes to change a process from the last good part of the previous batch to the first good part of the new batch (subtracting the cycle time used to produce the first part). An *element* is the smallest amount of work that can be moved to another process or person. *Internal elements* are elements that must be completed while the machine or process is shut down; for example, changing the stamping die. *External elements* are the elements that can be prepared or completed while the machine is operating; for example, inspecting and lubricating the next die to be used.

The idea behind the SMED methodology is to convert internal elements to external elements. This approach is beneficial when you have someone available to prepare the external elements while the machine is operating (normally, the operators have some time available). This method is highly recommended to reduce changeover time, thereby allowing you extra production time to increase output or build in smaller batches. The following is a brief overview of how the method works.

1. First, determine whether implementing SMED is appropriate for you. If you are experiencing the following, consider reducing your changeover time:
   - You are short of capacity.
   - The process is a bottleneck.
   - You need to change over more frequently (as is often the case in high-mix environments).
   - You need to reduce lead time (by changing over more frequently and working in smaller batches).
   - You need to increase on-time delivery.

   Even if you feel confident that your changeover times are optimum, consider the following:
   - You utilize only one operator to change over a machine. Consider making a second operator or team leader available to assist, especially if the process has a bottleneck.
   - Although prior to the changeover, you prepare tools, programs, and materials, and then physically change the machine efficiently, you spend considerable time making adjustments to the first few parts, even though you have manufactured these parts in the past. If this rings true for you, you may not be returning the machine to the same parameters used when you previously made this part, at the desired quality level. You have a changeover problem and should consider possible solutions discussed in this chapter.
   - After producing the first part, the machine sits waiting while the part is quality-checked and the documentation completed. Because you

have been manufacturing this part for years, however, a quality problem is probably not a concern. If the material is inexpensive compared to the value added by the machine, and if you know the program is good and the parameters are reasonably correct, quickly check the part for problems most likely to occur during setup (wrong tooling, wrong adjustments, and so on), and then start the machine running while completing the detailed quality check.

2. Observe a changeover by using the following methods:

- Videotape operators (focus on hand, body, and eye movements).
- Draw a spaghetti diagram (showing all operator's walking movements).
- List and time all elements completed by the operator.
- Review the items in Figure 5-1.

ADDITIONAL ITEMS TO REVIEW DURING SETUP
PLANNING
• Are tools, fixtures, etc., prepared (tool cart, belts, etc.)?   • Is standardized preparation list available? Does it include necessary information (technical specs) for particular part number?   • Is next material prepared?   • Are checklists available?   • Are tools, fixtures, etc. located in the best available place? Are they labeled?
BETTER TOOLING
• Is improved tooling available?   • Is faster tooling available? Combined tooling, air tools?   • Are better fixtures available? Quick-change?   • Is the machine designed for quick changeover?
WORKING METHOD
• Clear sequence or operator is unsure? Does standardized work exist?   • Which elements can be converted to external elements?   • Are all current working elements required, or is unnecessary work being performed?   • Reaching too far?   • Walking too far?   • Torques too tight?   • Is operator required to turn or reach?   • Does operator have difficultly finding items?   • Can more than one operator be involved in the changeover?   • Is it clear what to quality check and how?   • When the quality check indicates an out of standard condition, is there a reference sheet showing what adjustments should correct the problem? Are we making too many adjustments?   • How can adjustments be eliminated (or at least minimized)?

Figure 5-1. Items to be reviewed during a setup.

3. Separate movements into those elements currently performed internally and externally. Then identify those that can become external (see Figure 5-2).

4. Convert internal elements to external elements (starting with those that can be moved to external without significant cost).

5. Improve all aspects of the setup operation (reducing the necessary time).

Element	Current State		Future State		Necessary Steps	Investment Required
	Internal	External	Internal	External		
Get toolbox		3 min		3 min		
Get cutting tools		8 min		8 min		
Change tools into holders	15 min			15 min	Team leader to prepare	N/A
Remove previous tooling	8 min		6 min		Have tooling cart available to reduce walking	N/A
Lubricate new tooling	4 min			4 min	Team leader to prepare	N/A
Install prepared toolholders in machine	8 min		8 min			

Figure 5-2. Converting internal elements to external elements.

Also keep in mind the five most common problems and, therefore, opportunities to improve:

- Standardized changeover procedures are rarely followed; instead, the operator has a vague procedure in his mind that is the result of his and others' experiences. Instead of taking this approach, determine the best method for the highest quality and efficiency, standardize the work (in a written form), train all operators, and then follow up to verify the standards. Even if the situation involves frequent adjustments, create a standard sheet showing "when this is out of tolerance, adjust this."

- Hand tooling is awkward or wastes time. Eliminating or improving hand tooling is also a great opportunity for improvements that should be looked into in the following order:
  - Eliminate the need for a hand tool (wrenches and screwdrivers) by using quick clamps, quick fixtures, tooling incorporated into the machine, and so on.
  - Improve tooling by using electric or air tools, ratchet wrenches instead of box wrenches, and so on.
  - Put tooling in a better location (for example, a tool cart or a tool belt on the operator).

- Changeover time is not continuously monitored or recorded; therefore, managers and operators are unaware and not focused on its importance.

Treat changeover time just like any other process: Track it; use boards; and discuss any variance from the standard as soon as possible.

- Use common standard machine tooling instead of specialized tools where possible to reduce the number of machine tools requiring exchange during a setup, even at the sacrifice of slightly increasing the run time. Frequently in low volume, you spend more time changing and adjusting these specialized tools than you benefit in reducing the machining time.

- In most changeovers, 50 percent or more of the time involved is utilized for the adjustment phase. After a machine is producing a part to the desired quality level and you expect to produce this part again, record all the parameters utilized. In the future, you can quickly return the machine to this starting point. On older machines, work to reduce any point where variation can be introduced when returning to previous set points. Figure 5-3 shows one example of how to quickly return an older machine to the previous point at which it produced good parts.

These marks indicate setup positions for the various parts. They allow the operator to quickly return to that point. Sometimes color coding is also used for frequently produced parts.

Figure 5-3. Quickly returning a machine to previous parameters.

Often overlooked is the idea of having more then one operator (or the team leader) involved in performing the changeover. This should especially be considered for your bottleneck operations. Besides the obvious advantage of saving time by having more hands involved, this approach also forces management to standardize and balance the work. Just be sure the machine or process is large enough that two or more people can work together in the allocated space comfortably and safely, with an operator or team leader available to assist. When you separate the work elements and distribute them between the two people, keep the most difficult or detailed work with the regular operator; this will reduce the training required for the additional operator. Figure 5-4 illustrates an easy way to visualize who works on what and in which order—a timeline with common tasks shown in the middle.

Minutes	Machine operator	Work together	Helper
1	Disassemble Jaw 1		Disassemble Jaw 2
2			
3			
4	Move cart to machine		
5		Lift/install fixture	
6			
7			
8			
9	Change tools		Clean chips-critical area
10			
11			
12			
13			
14			Remove handtools from machine
15			
16	Load new program		
17	Adjust offsets		
18			

Figure 5-4. Two operators completing a changeover together.

In high-mix environments, you will not be able to observe and improve changeovers for each specific part number. Remember you want to stay process focused, not product focused; therefore you need to group your changeovers by type and then improve that "type" of changeover.

Also keep in mind, when considering future capital equipment expenditures in your low-volume business, that a machine designed for quick changeover is almost always going to save you more money than a machine with a fast process time (fast feeds and speeds). In high-volume manufacturing, this axiom isn't always true, but in low-volume, it is.

Increasing Machine Feeds and Speeds

Even in the most competent and technically sophisticated operations, there often exists the opportunity to increase the speed of the machine. Are new types of tooling available? Are current feeds and speeds maximized for the machine and tooling? There are two areas that are good candidates for improvement through increased feed or speed:

- Non-value-added time, such as indexing, positioning the part, ejecting the part, opening doors, and so on. Specific things to examine include the following:
  - Review pneumatic speeds for potential increases.
  - Design a better fixture.
  - Review machines internal PLC program for long delay times, extra processing time, and so on.
- Value-added time, such as cutting, forming, injecting, stamping, heating, welding, and so on. Specific things to consider include the following:
  - If programs were developed internally, have their logic and speeds checked by another programmer for a second opinion.
  - Tooling or machine consumables should be frequently reviewed and compared with newly available products.

Bottleneck Analysis

When you ask a supervisor, "What is your bottleneck process?" the response is either quite specific ("CNC #2") or quite vague ("It depends"). On occasion, it might even be "What's a bottleneck?"

In high-volume plants, a bottleneck can be easily determined if visual buffers have predetermined sizes. If a buffer before the process is full and the one after is empty, the process is likely a bottleneck. If the buffer before is nearly empty and the one after is full, the process that follows is probably the bottleneck.

In low-volume plants, however, bottlenecks may be far less clear. The first thing to do, then, is to gather some data to clarify the situation or discover whether/how the bottleneck changes depending on certain measurable or quantifiable conditions.

In Figure 5-5, we can assume that these are random processes identified as possible bottlenecks and they manufacture various products, and that the materials do not necessarily flow from one to the next machine.

Study during _4_ shifts or ____ hours

Processes identified as possible bottlenecks ==>	Grinder 224	CNC 678	Drill 321	Drill 964
Total wait time (no part available from previous processes)	300"	45"	3309"	2021"
Total holding time (buffer after the process is full, following processes slow/stopped)	0"	199"	400"	6077"
Planned cycle time	130"	120"	145"	108"
Average & high cycle times during observation	133", 155"	151", 277"	149", 170"	108", 139"

Figure 5-5. Analysis of perceived bottlenecks.

- The CNC 678 could be a problem because the average cycle time is considerably more than the planned cycle time, and if the workload was planned for 120 seconds and it is actually taking 151 seconds (on the average), that difference might be causing waiting time at the next process.

- Although someone thought Drill 321 was a bottleneck, it seems the process (or possibly multiple processes) supplying this drill is the real problem, because a lot of waiting time is involved.

- Drill 964 also seems to wait periodically, although it has a short process time and appears to catch up quickly and fill the buffer to the following process or processes. The problem could have to do with the balance between this drill and the later processes.

The figure illustrates that it is not always easy to understand where the bottleneck in a low-volume shop is located. The bottleneck site may even change, depending on many factors within the operations and on customer demand for various products. A corollary to this is that it is somewhat difficult to set up a simple system that will reveal the bottleneck(s) in a low-volume environment.

One inexpensive idea that has worked well is to put an inexpensive, battery-operated wall clock on those processes you believe are bottlenecks. This can help gather data that can help you determine whether these areas are actually bottlenecks due to downtime or a bottleneck caused by the difference in capacity versus demand. There are two methods to do this (see Figure 5-6):

- **Manually operated downtime clock:** Insert a switch between the battery and the contacts on the clock then set the clock to 12:00. Instruct the operator to turn on the switch each time the process is down and turn it off only after the process starts again. The supervisor should then reset the clock to 12:00 at the end of each shift and record the total downtime for the shift. In the example given in Figure 5-6, there is approximately five minutes of accumulated downtime (the clock reads 12:05) at the end of the shift.

- **Automatically operated downtime clock:** You approach this method the same way as with the manually operated clock, except instead of connecting to a switch, you connect to a normally open relay inside the machine. This should be a relay that closes contact whenever the machine is abnormally stopped (for example, when the machine's red warning light would normally be turned on). The clock is also reset to 12:00 at the beginning of each shift.

Manually Operated Downtime Clock   Automatically Operated Downtime Clock

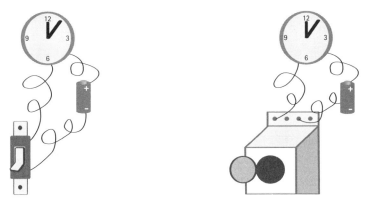

Figure 5-6. Simple method of bottleneck analysis.

The data recorded by the supervisor indicates which processes have the most downtime. Those that are already scheduled near capacity and have significant downtime are probably your bottlenecks.

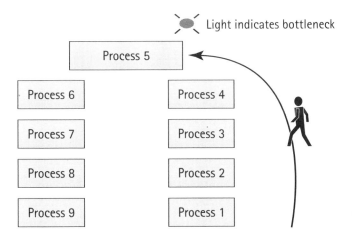

Figure 5-7. Making the bottleneck visual.

Once you identify the bottleneck, set up a visual method to make everyone aware of it. This could be a sign board or light (see Figure 5-7) you move to the process to indicate where it currently is. This visual indicator should help the operators, managers, and the team leaders focus on reducing stops on this process. (Andon lights, another tool for helping reduce bottlenecks, are discussed in chapter 9.)

Machine Performance (Overall Equipment Effectiveness)

When working to increase output, how your machine (or process) is performing is critical. Many companies measure the utilization, output, and quality of a process separately—a stamping machine's performance, for example, may be measured as utilization of 75 percent, output of 80 percent, and quality of 90 percent. These numbers taken by themselves are usually not a concern, though if you look at the combined effect, you receive a good part only 54 percent of the total time ($75\% \times 80\% \times 90\% = 54\%$). Now, you might want to be concerned.

This is the idea behind overall equipment effectiveness (OEE): It is a measurement that includes *all* losses that can occur on a machine or process. It is a standardized measurement that removes allowances. Many companies fool themselves by having uptime measurements that include many allowances. They may even have an industrial engineer calculate these allowances, and this individual, after removing any disturbances he or she feels are uncontrollable, is the only one who truly knows what has been included and excluded. Either approach leaves management with a nice, comfortable number but hides numerous problems.

On the other hand, OEE = Availability(%) × Performance(%) × Quality(%), and by calculating this cumulative number, you call attention to the processes with the most significant opportunities. Naturally, you want to focus on any bottleneck processes with low OEE. You can then break down the reasons for the percentages being low and prioritize an action plan. You can also use OEE to help you decide where other lean tools like TPM (total productive maintenance) should be focused.

In a low-volume environment, frequent changeovers will show a lower availability for a machine, and scrap losses during changeovers will further reduce performance. Because both availability and performance are part of the OEE equation, the machine will quickly become the focus of attention. (More detail on how to apply OEE is found in chapter 10.)

Standardized Work

Standardized work is, by definition, the most efficient method of producing the best quality. Standardizing work is necessary for all critical and repetitive processes. The following is a list of only a few of the reasons that standardized work is so important:

74

- It is the baseline for improvements (without a standard method, you have no basis from which to *kaizen*; that is, continuously improve).

- It is currently the best method for maintaining quality and efficiency (therefore, it should increase output).

- It is a management tool that enables seeing normal versus abnormal conditions.

Some examples of standardized work in high-volume plants are shown in Figure 5-8, which shows a typical machining cell worksheet and a combination table showing the relationship in time between an automatic machine cycle

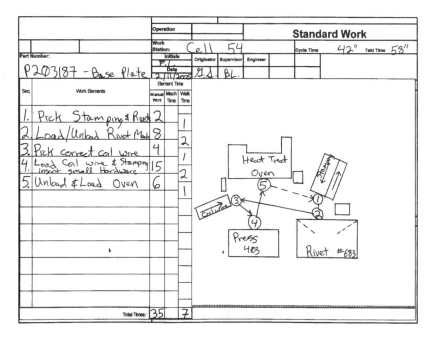

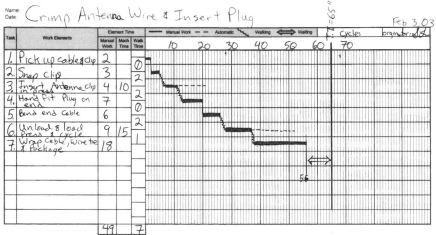

Figure 5-8. Traditional standardized work and combination table from a high-volume plant.

and manual work. Figure 5-9 shows detailed manual operations that are better understood with pictures.

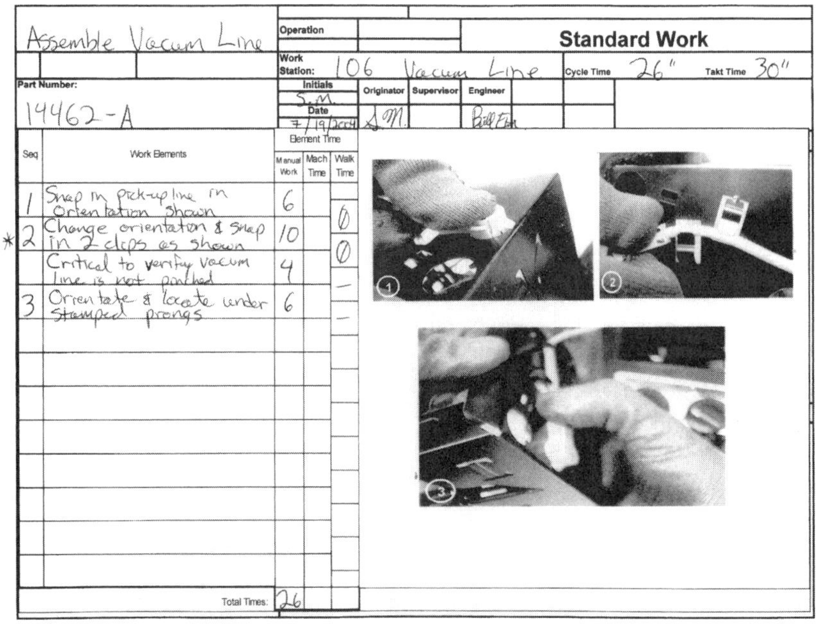

Figure 5-9. Standardized work for a manual operation.

Despite its undisputed importance, however, standardized work is a difficult subject to handle in high-mix, low-volume plants. In fact, if a low-volume plant were to try to complete typical work standards for all its parts and processes with methods similar to those used in high-volume plants, creating and analyzing all the necessary documentation might lead to bankruptcy. Some options for choosing which processes require work standards in high-mix, low-volume plants are listed below:

- Choose the top 20 percent of your highest running parts and develop work standards for each type or category of part in this group (assuming this is a feasible quantity).

- Group parts into *product families* (a group of products that pass through similar process steps or common machines) and issue one work standard per family (if one standard can represent a family).

- Write general work standards for procedures such as setups, inspections, assembling, and so on, and use day-by-hour charts to encourage standard and efficient processes (this applies especially to job shops).

- If only certain work steps are the same, but the entire sequence differs, divide the parts into work elements, group similar work elements together, and define a standard method and time for each of these elements. Then develop a database to link each part number to its standardized work elements, so that, as individual parts are required, operators can access those work standards that are necessary for that part. The database would contain work standards (one document for each element) for each different work element associated with a part number.

Another possibility is to complete work standards only as problems or needs are identified. For example, even if you start out without any work standards, when you have a quality problem because of an incorrect work sequence, or because a step was forgotten, write and post the standard. If you find a process being done differently by two operators or discover an inefficient process sequence, write the standard. If a new tool or piece of equipment is purchased, write the standards for how to use it. This will require developing a format first; then, as you identify the processes in need of work standards, you have a template for documenting your findings. (Guidelines for writing standardized work for low-volume parts are presented in chapter 9.)

Dedicated Material Handlers

Having skilled operators restock their own material in the work area is typical in high-mix, low-volume plants. This is an item for improvement, especially in busy times. Why lose capacity by having experienced operators performing restocking work that anyone can do? Skilled operators should have a dedicated material handler bringing their material, tools, and consumables. Using a material handler requires a communication system prior to the material running out, such as a two-bin system, a card system, or a simple list. During slow times, this responsibility can be rebalanced to the skilled operator, and the less skilled material handler can be reassigned elsewhere. Two generic prerequisites to separate this work follow; these may not apply to every business:

- Bills of materials (BOM) must be in place.
- Planning systems, indicating which materials are required prior to their being needed.

  When considering dedicated material handlers, you must clearly define which method of part delivery and storage you will utilize:
  - *Kitting material*
  - *Line-side storage*
  - *A Combination of kitting material with some line-side storage*

Kitting material is another strategy employed in high-mix, low-volume environments. With kitting, some (or all) of the material necessary to complete work orders is grouped together prior to starting production. Frequently, this can be done in combination with line-side storage, stocking only smaller or frequently used parts at the line where they are used (for example, small hardware, standard fittings). In a high-mix environment, kitting has the advantage of both the person kitting and the operator checking that the correct parts are being used, reducing quality problems. Parts that are used in various locations throughout the plant are also candidates for kitting. Kitting reduces lineside storage space, wasteful walking, and quality problems (though it adds some double handling to processes).

It is best to kit parts only when necessary, but kitting is common in low-volume plants where large variations in part types make it difficult to store all the variants in a single assembly area. A hybrid solution is storing common parts and small hardware (screws, O-rings, and so on) beside the line, and kitting the other material. This hybrid approach also makes managing the line easier, as only the people kitting are moving throughout the plant—the assembly operators are at their workstations, instead of walking around looking for materials.

Team Leaders

A team leader is an hourly paid person, generally promoted from within the team, who has the following responsibilities:

- Provide assistance to primary operator:
  - Answer andon calls for assistance
  - Troubleshoot tooling problems
  - Determine when to call maintenance and who should respond (mechanical or electrical)
  - Perform or assist with changeovers
  - Execute pull systems
  - Handle defective material
  - Measure and track results
  - Provide emergency relief
- Provide coverage for operator absenteeism
- Follow and procure material when needed
- Keep records associated with overtime work
- Assist area supervisor to ensure proper rotation concepts
- Perform training and maintain training documentation (manage visual boards)
- Perform process monitoring (for each process and operator)
- Perform quality audits
- Provide input and monitor conformance to TPM procedures/schedules
- Provide input to root cause analysis

- Provide documentation for machine problems/downtime causes
- Assist supervisor to ensure proper scheduling of production
- Assist supervisor to ensure timely and accurate completion of vacation schedules
- Assist supervisor in maintaining department supplies and indirect materials

If you are unsure of how this position helps with increasing output, you probably haven't worked with good team leaders! For managers working in corporate cultures—who think in terms of direct and indirect employees—team leaders might be considered "indirect" personnel who cannot be cost justified. But consider the following additional contributions of a team leader and how each can increase output:

- Fills in for absent operators, minimizing lost production
- Reduces lost production when operators (who are untrained in problem resolution) handle their own problems
- Resolves all problems in his or her team, quantifying where the largest problems are generated and keeping management focused
- Has the time and ability to put in place permanent countermeasures for reoccurring problems

Also remember that many of the most efficient manufacturing plants in the world use team leaders. Without them, you will have a difficult time implementing other lean concepts, such as andon, balance walls, effective changeovers, day-by-hour boards, and cross training. Also, without team leaders, who handles the problem solving?

The Problem with Problem Solving

For many managers, it is normal to encourage workers to try to resolve problems on their own before calling for help, but the problems remain hidden and usually unsolved at their root. Many low-volume plants have built-in timeslots for operators to solve problems. In other words, you assign an operator a job, walk away, and assume when he or she encounters a problem, the operator will fix it and let you know about it. The underlying assumption is that everyone is a reasonable problem-solver and will go about doing their tasks efficiently. Many of these plants, even some who have nominally adopted lean, load operators to only 75 percent or 80 percent, knowing problems will arise and take up the remaining time and focus.

The lean approach is to load operators to 95 percent. When problems arise, the operators hand them over to a problem-solving specialist—the team leader—and begin working on the next order. Remember, as well, that the best team leaders are promoted from within the company, from among your current operators, without increasing your headcount.

Outsourcing

After reviewing the seven improvement ideas in this chapter and implementing some (or all) of them to increase capacity, you may still find yourself in need of outsourcing. Some levels in the organization see outsourcing as a simple activity, though most organizations encounter significant problems, for example, not having updated their drawings during the years they have been manufacturing this part, or having developed special methods and tooling to simplify manufacturing which are unknown to others, all of which involves time and cost to develop within a supplier.

Which products you decide to outsource should not be selected arbitrarily; this section provides some guidelines. But before outsourcing any products because of capacity issues, you should consider the following questions:

- Are these products you should be making in the first place (see the make-versus-buy flow chart in Figure 5-10)?

- Are there other products consuming capacity from this process that you should be buying instead of making?

- Are there other options that have been overlooked? Additional shifts? Using other machines or processes? Hiring temporary labor? Overtime?

The flow chart in Figure 5-10 can be used to evaluate making or buying an item from a strategic standpoint. Once the make-versus-buy decision has been reviewed for all part numbers running on a particular process, and you remove those that the make-versus-buy flow chart indicates should be purchased, ensure that all other options to create extra capacity have been exhausted if a shortage of capacity still exists. This includes all the methods discussed in this chapter: changeover time reduction; machine feed and speed increases; bottleneck analysis; machine performance; work standards; dedicated material handlers; and team leaders. You might also have the opportunity to operate this process on additional shifts, offload some work to another machine or process, or use temporary labor to absorb some of the related manual work.

Only after all of these options are exhausted should you proceed (with caution) to outsource parts that you would normally manufacture. The following are just some of the related issues you need to consider:

- For what length of time do you believe outsourcing is necessary (based on accuracy of forecasts from your customers)?

- What are the startup costs—tooling; fixtures; capital investment; and so on?

- Should you allow the supplier to use some of your excess tooling or fixtures?
- What is your commitment to the supplier if the forecast changes?
- What costs are the supplier's responsibility if there is poor quality or a late delivery?

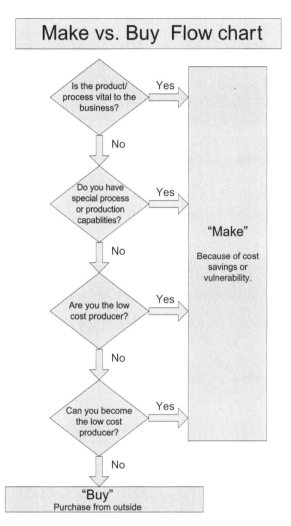

Figure 5-10. Make-versus-buy flow chart.

Finally, if you find yourself in the position of purchasing additional equipment to create capacity, be sure you take the necessary steps to purchase only flexible equipment. Remember, you may currently be short of capacity for manufacturing this particular part, but still have excess capacity for similar parts—this can be the result of having purchased inflexible equipment. So that you do not find yourself in a similar situation as customer requirements change, see chapter 6.

Summary of Key Points

- Certain products should be purchased instead of manufactured; use the make-versus-buy flow chart to determine those products.

- Outsourcing because you are short of capacity should not be the first step; instead, the seven ideas discussed in this chapter should be looked into first (to create additional capacity):
    - Reduce changeover times
    - Review machine parameters (increasing feeds and speeds)
    - Do a bottleneck analysis
    - Increase machine OEE
    - Use standardized work
    - Use dedicated material handlers
    - Use team leaders

- When outsourcing parts you would normally manufacture, ensure a sound strategy.

- If you decide to purchase equipment to increase your capacity, purchase only flexible equipment (also see chapter 6).

- Any time you change a person's working method, you temporarily have some slow cycle times while the operator learns the new method.

- Remember to write work standards for any processes you change or any new processes you put in place.

6

Making Improvements When You Have Excess Capacity

When your capacity (equipment and staff) exceeds your customer's demand, and you are unable to sell the excess capacity profitably, you need quick actions to reduce your costs and stay competitive. Your options are based on the following parameters:

- How long you are forecast to have excess capacity
- The skill level required in your industry
- Labor laws
- Union relations

With any luck, when you find yourself in this situation, you have the following in place and up to date:

- Standardized work for office processes
- Standardized work for operations in production
- Visualization to show workload in the office
- Visualization to show workload on the shop floor:
  - Day-by-hour or FIFO boards
  - Work balance walls in any areas of higher volume or standard products (*work balance walls* are bar charts used to compare operator workload and show the relationship of workload to takt time when applicable)

If these visual aids or their equivalents are not in place, you are not in a position to understand how reduced sales are affecting individual workloads; therefore, you cannot begin rebalancing work and reducing costs. However, given your extra capacity, you now have extra manpower available to put together this missing standardization and visualization.

If you take no action during a down period, your costs will stay the same while your income decreases. To capture any savings, you need some analysis and action tools. The chart in Figure 6-1 shows typical workload in the office or shop environment that is experiencing a slow period. Note that it may be difficult to observe the downtime directly or accurately because employees may continue to look busy.

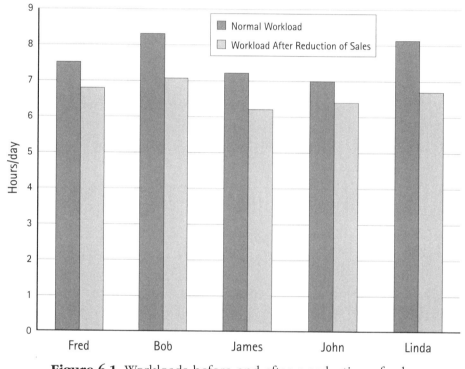

Figure 6-1. Workloads before and after a reduction of sales.

Generally, in low-volume plants, you have a higher percentage of overhead/staff costs because you have more indirect office work associated with each small order (material procurement, order intake, sales, engineering, order scheduling, and so on). Because staff in low-volume plants is typically the last to be let go in slow times (they are often difficult to replace), these plants are more directly affected by sales slumps and the situation shown in Figure 6-1 is often tolerated during these slump periods. The next few sections discuss some lean techniques that can be applied in these situations, both in office processes and on the shop floor.

In the Office

We can begin this discussion with two basic techniques for the office. Each of these addresses the issue of utilizing human resources more effectively, especially during slow periods.

Having Sufficient Standardized Operations and Cross-Training in Place

If your office operates on a *knowledge basis* (that is, a few key people have most of the information in their heads) instead of being based on documented procedures, you have created a dangerous situation that constantly puts your business at risk. Consider what can occur if any of your key people take a vacation, are sick, or leave the company. If they take their knowledge with them, things will fall into disarray.

The first thing you need to do to remove your business from this chronic high-risk condition is put together a skills matrix that shows the current situation (see Figure 6-2 on page 22).

In this matrix (also called a cross-training matrix), each critical office process is identified, along with the individual(s) qualified to perform the process and to what extent they are trained is indicated by the number of quadrants filled in within the circle. You can see at a glance if only one person has been trained to perform a process; for example, Roger Moore is the only person fully capable of performing "Place Purchase Orders for Nonstock Items." This is obviously a major concern; if Roger is incapacitated or retires, there currently is no other person capable of performing this work. Moreover, the section of the grid indicating "status of cross training" (near the bottom of the matrix) is marked red/yellow/green to show the high-risk level of this situation—no one is being trained to do this work!

The same chart provides additional useful information. It can be used for numerous purposes, and uses symbols to accentuate significant issues that require additional or immediate attention. In this example, the circle with the four quadrants is shaded within a green box to highlight where training is planned and to what level, and red/yellow/green is used to identify the status of having "standardized operations" complete and documented.

If you do not have a similar chart for your organization, you should consider creating one as soon as possible. Moreover, your chart should involve and include input from every department. Each department can start with a blank chart and fill it in as completely and as accurately as possible. (Note that certain information may need to be filled in or modified later.) Next, combine the charts so that you have one for the entire office. With this information in place, you can immediately begin cross-training people to perform functions in various departments.

If your sales are slow, it is likely that people have time on their hands. This is a good time to write the standardized operations/work documents and cross-train. The matrix can help you prioritize these activities and track progress. It also allows you to evaluate options during slow periods. You can clearly see your most skilled people (for example, Roger Moore) and what cross-training would be required if you terminate some of your less skilled employees (for example, Beverly Jones). Displaying the filled-in matrix serves to make everyone in a given department aware of work or processes that are "covered" and those that are "at-risk." Employees can also see what they are capable of compared with others, as well as what training plans are in the works. Some companies decide not to display these matrixes because of perceived apprehensions from some employees.

Having Only Skilled Employees Performing Skilled Tasks

Most jobs involve tasks that require both higher and lower skill levels, and this presents an excellent opportunity to separate the tasks and assign them to different people during slow times. This is especially true in an office, where many tasks are now completed with computers.

Refer back to Figure 6-1 and assume that each of the employees in the office can separate their daily tasks into those that require special skill or special knowledge and those that can be performed by a less skilled person. The result can then be presented as shown in Figure 6-3.

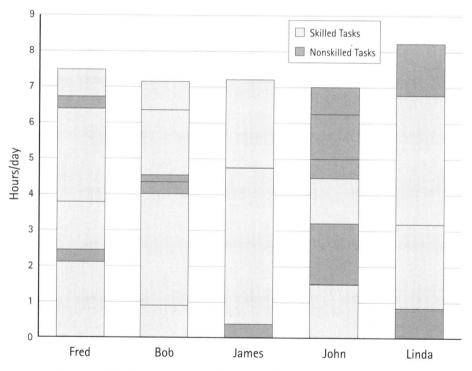

Figure 6-3. Work separated into skilled and nonskilled tasks.

If we further assume that John leaves the company for some reason, we can train Fred and Linda to perform his skilled tasks and move everyone's nonskilled tasks to an administrative person (this person could be an internal transfer or a new hire at a lower pay level). Obviously, this requires writing work standards for the nonskilled tasks and training the new hire. The immediate savings is only the difference between John's pay and the administrative person's pay level, but additional savings will accrue over time.

If we now have the work separated (skilled and nonskilled) as shown in Figure 6-4, we have more options. For example, assume the company experiences a 20 percent sales reduction, and this equates to a 15 percent average workload reduction. We now have the hours/day shown in Figure 6-5, where everyone experiences some slowdown.

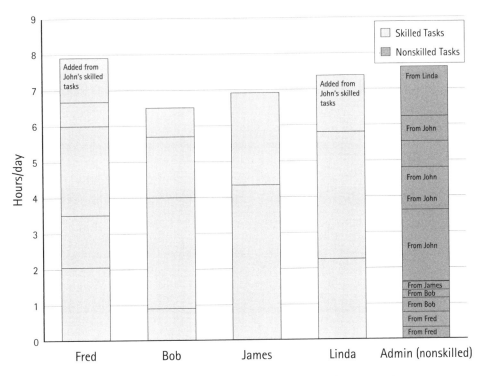

Figure 6-4. All nonskilled work moved to an administrative person.

Now the office is in a position for a simple rebalancing of the nonskilled tasks back to the skilled operators that previously performed them as shown in Figure 6-6. This flexibility allows a 20 percent manpower reduction (one of five employees). And if the administrative person is working on a temporary contract, these changes are even easier for the organization to accept.

On the Shop Floor

It was previously mentioned that your options are based on the forecasted period you will have excess capacity, the difficulty of finding and training new

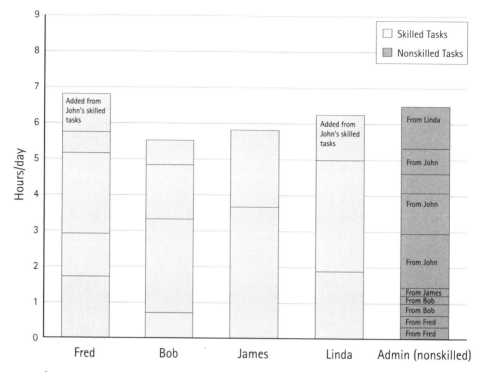

Figure 6-5. All nonskilled work moved to an administrative person, and a general workload reduction caused by a sales decrease.

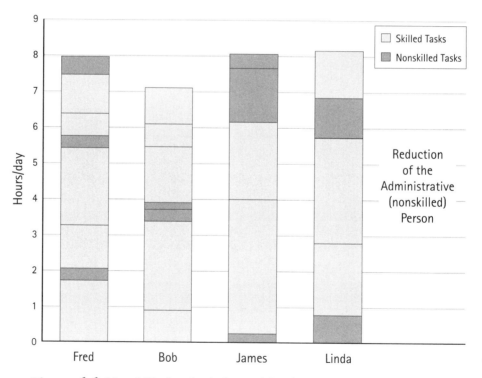

Figure 6-6. Nonskilled tasks balanced back to skilled team members.

employees if demand increases (that is, the skill level and training time necessary and the number of procedures you have documented), the laws in your country regarding layoffs/terminations, and your working relationship with a union.

The focus here will be limited only to "the difficulty of finding and training new employees" as the other factors are shaped by your particular industry, experience, and situation. As previously noted, most companies put themselves in a dangerous situation by relying too heavily on the knowledge in the heads of individual employees. This makes training new employees difficult, because it promotes an inadequate documentation of processes. The smaller your business, the more dangerous this situation becomes, because each person is more critical and is responsible for a wider range of processes. Some of you reading this statement may be thinking, "We are proud of the fact that we have experienced employees who are trusted to do many things," and, on some levels, you have every right to feel this way. Great employees are the backbone of all successful companies. The point here is that one employee's illness or departure should not be permitted to shut down your company. You have unique processes, practices, and machinery in your business that few others outside your company have experience with, so you cannot afford to put your company at risk by too much dependence on any one employee, no matter how skilled and trustworthy he or she is.

For example, a machine shop can hire a graduate machinist who has worked in firms using similar materials and has even manufactured similar parts, but rarely will this person be familiar with the exact machinery, methods, and unique procedures that have made this company successful. Even if you are hiring this person to help you find new and improved methods, he or she will need to understand how you are currently operating; moreover, production must continue while changes are being implemented. Therefore, the more you document specific procedures, the quicker you can bring new employees up to speed.

The documentation can be captured as standardized work (the current best method for quality and efficiency) or can be assembled and presented in another format. Standardized work is a difficult concept to get your mind around in a low-volume environment because of the scope of products and procedures utilized, but grouping similar products into families and utilizing some of the methods mentioned in this chapter can facilitate this task. (The range of format options for this will be briefly discussed in chapter 9.)

Some readers may find the concept of documenting work standards intimidating. Typical reasons for this include the following:

- We have employees with many years of service and stable customers; we're not going to be blindsided.
- The people who know these specific processes are busy and do not necessarily have good documentation skills.

- This is a lot of work in our business, with all the various products and processes.

- We have too many specialized processes.

- This will cost a lot, and we will lose productivity during implementation.

If you find yourself thinking about the first point (having longevity with employees and stable customers) and believing this secures your future, think of upcoming retirements, unexpected events in people's lives (like illness or injury), events not forecasted for industries, and changes in relationships with your customers (for example, new management, buyouts, new buyers, competitors).

Fortunately, there are some easy ways to come to terms with each of the points listed above. Remember that periods of excess capacity mean that most employees have free time available each day. You can use some of this time to document processes, thereby safeguarding your future.

The first step is to complete a skills matrix (like the one in Figure 6-7) for the different areas of the shop floor to help identify your critical processes and your current skill levels within these processes. Make sure to fill in the red/yellow/green areas to indicate the "status of standardized operations." If there is no documentation available, the process is red; if there is some form of documentation but it is incomplete, the process is yellow; and if the documentation is complete and at an acceptable level, it is green.

Also complete the matrix **R** **Y** **G** for the "status of cross-training." If only one person is currently capable of performing the task, the status is red; if only two people are capable, it is yellow; otherwise, it is green.

Once these factors have been evaluated and filled in, you can use the data indicated by "status of the standardized work" and the "status of cross-training" to prioritize a plan for documentation (you can use the same data to evaluate whether your training plan is adequate). For example, **R** and **R** indicate a top priority (for example, in Figure 6-7, "Building manifold subassemblies for low pressure" is one of the top priorities). **R** and **Y** indicate a second priority (for example, in Figure 6-7, "Building manifold subassemblies for high pressure"), and so on.

Next, decide which type of documentation to use.

1. **Make a video of the process.** This is the quickest way to document your processes. It is also good for training. The operator should explain the steps and the peculiarities of the process during the videotaping. These videos are lifesavers if nobody with knowledge of the process is available to perform it.

2. **Write major process steps and attach digital pictures for clarification.** You can choose from a number of formats to use for this task

(some examples are shown in chapter 9), but it is important to define the purpose of the document you plan to use before choosing a format. For example, will the process document also be used as a quality document? Should it contain technical specifications? Should it contain the time to complete the process? These are important questions, because you might want to use a single document for multiple purposes (e.g., training, setting quality standards, capturing the necessary time to complete the task, and so on).

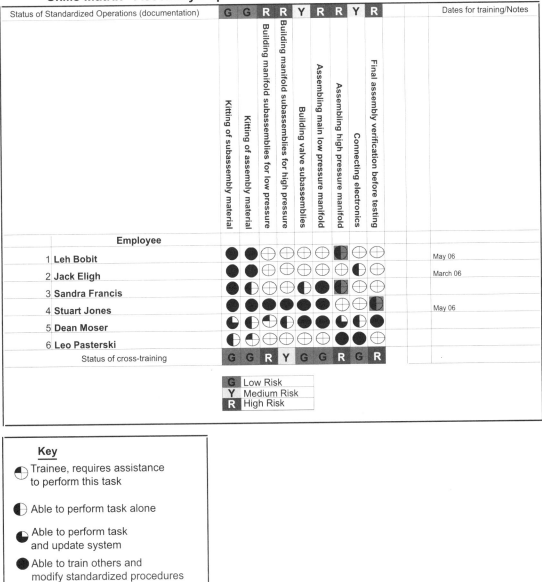

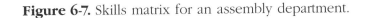

Figure 6-7. Skills matrix for an assembly department.

3. Decide how general or specific a process the document will describe.

If you are writing the document to capture a process involving a product, you need to decide which products follow similar steps and how many of those products you can group into a family, and then write the documentation for an entire family.

To Reduce the Excess Capacity

There are many ways to reduce the excess capacity in your plant. Some (or all) of those presented below may be appropriate for your business.

Reducing the Number of Temporaries

Temporary employees that have entered your labor force through an agency are usually the first to go during slow times. While letting good temporary people go is a sacrifice, there are times when it must be done for the good of the business. It is always good policy to give agency temps some advance notice of the impending layoff; this is generally not required, but it is a courteous gesture that can work to your advantage. The immediate advantage is that the temp worker will be more willing to train the permanent employee who will be reassigned to the job. In the best case scenario, this individual may even be open to sharing information about changes or improvements he or she has implemented on the job tasks. This is also a particularly good time for the employee who will assume the temp's responsibilities to document any critical processes, including any new procedures or methods the temp has been using.

Having Operators Do Unskilled Tasks

During busy times, skilled operators should perform only skilled tasks. They should never be assigned to unskilled tasks like getting material, obtaining tools, cleaning machines, and so on. This work can be performed by others. When work slows down, however, the skilled operator can be assigned to unskilled tasks, and the material handler or the machine cleaner can be laid off or reassigned elsewhere. (If you have somewhat more repetitive processes, you can rebalance with balancing walls, which are discussed in chapter 9.)

Smoothing the Workload

One reason for having excess capacity is uneven workload caused by customer fluctuations. Applying a combined kanban and work order board or the FIFO board (as discussed in chapter 4) will help you visualize the workload, smooth the fluctuations, and identify where too much capacity/manpower is available.

This also helps you to avoid overtime when a temporary spike in demand occurs during a downturn.

Another good way to smooth workload is to work with your customers and encourage them to accept split delivery dates on larger orders. This allows you to produce in smaller batches, which has many advantages besides smoothing the workload.

Purchasing Flexible Machinery

When you are experiencing excess capacity, you are often also dealing with inflexibility. One reason for this is the highly automated and inflexible machinery you have purchased. Many western countries with high labor costs get caught in the trap of buying highly automated machinery. While this machinery is fast and requires little labor, it is inflexible, has lower OEE (or uptime), and is costly when not being fully utilized. When customer demand changes, you cannot reduce the cost or utilize the machine's resources for other products.

Many company managers forget to consider the operator's standardized work before deciding on the level of automation to purchase. They spend money to overautomate, and then pay little attention to poorly balanced operators, who frequently stand around observing machines in operation.

As Figure 6-8 shows, you can have either extreme when purchasing new machinery: a completely manual process (level #1) or a complex machine that completely processes the part (level #3). The level #3 machines usually load and transfer a part automatically from one automatic process to another, require little involvement from operators, have little flexibility, require a lot of support from technicians, and can stop the process completely when one component breaks down.

Not surprisingly, there are some who view the level #3 machines as crossing the "great divide" into a condition that is overautomated. One disadvantage of overautomation is that the OEE (overall equipment effectiveness = availability $\times$ performance $\times$ quality) is usually lower on complicated or coupled machines. For example, if each of three connected machines have individual OEEs of 95%, the overall OEE = 95% $\times$ 95% $\times$ 95% = 85.7%. Once one machine is stopped, the entire process is stopped, although decoupling (with flexible processes) increases the OEE. Moreover, these highly automated machines require more skilled technicians, an additional expense. And watch out for the final reason for overautomating: people's fascination with technology, which causes them to lose focus of flexibility.

In contrast, the lean philosophy on acquiring capital equipment involves balancing quality, cost, flexibility, and well-balanced operations. In low-volume operations, machinery that is designed for quick set-up is more critical than

Level		Load	Process #1 (value add)	Unload	Load	Process #2 (value add)	Unload	Characteristics
1	Manual processes	🧍	🧍	🧍	🧍	🧍	🧍	• very flexible • no investment • need standard work to ensure quality
2	Flexible process	🧍	Auto	Auto	🧍	Auto	Auto	• flexible • medium investment • good quality
				Crossing the Great Divide				
3	Over-automated	Auto	Auto	Auto	Auto	Auto	Auto	• inflexible (transfer by robot) • high investment • poor OEE • good quality

Figure 6-8. Automation levels.

equipment that has fast cycle times (faster feeds and speeds). This should be a key consideration when specifying and purchasing new equipment.

A flexible process (level #2) should be your target. Generally, you will get good quality, stay competitively priced, and have flexibility with the man and machine when the customer demand increases or decreases. In this flexible process, the operator will perform tasks that would be costly to automate and do not require automation to ensure quality. The automated portion of work is performed by a simple machine that is flexible and can be easily used for other products. The operator is given enough work to ensure that he or she is well utilized.

In some cases, the operator can perform some of the steps on a semi-manual machine, especially if the family of parts has various specifications that can be handled outside the automatic machine. It is also ideal if the operator loads the automatic machine, because this balances him or her with the machine's cycle, although simple modifications may allow the machine to unload or eject the part. If you have to choose, remember that most parts need to be precisely located when a machine is being loaded, and this is expensive; when ejecting a part, placement is less critical and therefore much less expensive. Having a machine that ejects parts makes it easy for the operator to get and load a new part.

As noted above, operators should be well utilized and perform work that is well balanced. If work volumes change, it is much easier to rebalance an operator than to reprogram or change a machine. (How to rebalance is discussed in Chapter 9.)

Summary of Key Points

- Don't wait until your business slows down, but continuously update the following:
    - Standardized work for office processes
    - Standardized work for operations in production
    - Visualization to show workload in the office
    - Visualization to show workload on the shop floor
- Complete a skills matrix and document the critical processes.
- Document your processes so you are not vulnerable if key people leave the organization.
- To reduce excess capacity, first reduce the number of temporaries, and then rebalance and smooth the workload.
- Create flexibility by having all nonskilled work performed by nonskilled operators during busy times and rebalance to eliminate the nonskilled operators (material handlers, machine cleaners) in slow times.
- Try not to purchase inflexible machinery or develop inflexible processes, and pay attention to the standardized work of the operators when looking into new equipment..
- Write work standards for any processes you change or any new processes you put in place.

7

Using Value Stream Mapping in a Low-Volume Environment

Value stream mapping, although it is not a complete flow analysis, is a graphic tool that uses symbols to show the flow of material and information within your business. In a manufacturing environment you choose a key product (a *runner*) or key part number to map; in complicated processes, you might start with following only a subassembly or component that has significant costs. The map presents a picture of the process at a certain point in time; it is based on the actual situation on the shop floor instead of data retrieved from a database and it includes all manufacturing activities and the information flow of the incoming order. With value stream mapping, you are mapping the flow from raw material to the customer, including all the value- and non-value-added processes.

This tool highlights many improvement opportunities—most significantly, lead-time reductions. Because lead times affect cost and on-time delivery most directly, value stream mapping is recommended as the first tool to use when you begin work on reducing cost (after you have good quality levels and are meeting your required outputs). In low volume, it is difficult to start value stream mapping too early because the non-value-added time (time that material sits and waits usually as WIP) varies considerably depending on the current lead time, workload, capacity, etc. Therefore, it is better to begin by putting in day-by-hour and FIFO boards that will help control this and better quantify it, simplifying the drawing and understanding of the current state value stream map.

Getting Started

When mapping a process, you follow two flows:

- Material from door to door
- Information flow of the customer order through scheduling the production

Symbols are used to represent both lean and nonlean concepts. For example, when you are mapping your process and find that the supermarket or kanban symbol best represents your flow, most likely you are utilizing lean ideas. On the other hand, if you find that the inventory or push symbols represent your situation, you likely have opportunities for improvement (see Figure 7-1). (Remember in high mix you are not going to "pull" much of your material; instead you are going to "push" at the first process and then try to flow. Though since much of this flow is represented with either push symbols or ideally by FIFO symbols during value stream mapping, you should not be overly concerned by the use of the push symbol).

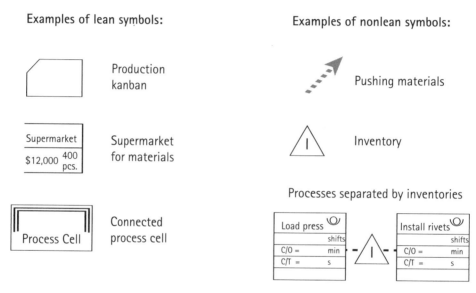

Figure 7-1. Lean and nonlean value stream mapping symbols.

The same concept holds true for information flow. For example, too many arrows from production control to the production processes demonstrate that you are separately scheduling each process. This indicates a need for improvement; because all this traditional scheduling is costly; instead you should be using FIFO and day-by-hour boards that require less effort from production control.

Total Product Cycle Time

Value stream mapping reduces cost by reducing lead time. The measurement for lead time is referred to as *total product cycle time* (TPCT), which measures the longest path from the receipt of raw material until it is shipped as a finished good. You also include the cost of the various inventories along the value stream to ensure that you do not concentrate on a path that does not have significant financial savings. The map also helps you visualize where most of your inventory is being held: for example in raw materials, work-in-process, or finished goods. If we extrapolate from this explanation, it is clear that reducing TPCT has several benefits:

- Reduced inventory
- Short lead time
- Better customer satisfaction

Value stream mapping is not only applicable to production, but can also be adapted and applied to other areas:

- Design and development processes
- Paperwork processes
- Service companies

Note: This chapter will specifically discuss V.S. mapping as it is applied in manufacturing processes, a similar tool called process mapping will be discussed in chapters 11 and 12 with relation to office processes.

Not only will you improve TPCT, but mapping highlights many opportunities within the seven types of waste. (The seven wastes, based on Toyota's experience, are correction, overproduction, motion, material movement, waiting, inventory, and over-processing. These can be easily be remembered by the abbreviation COMM WIP.)

At this point it is interesting to clarify some lean terminology. "Lead time" is often casually used though there are different types with significantly different meanings. For example, customer lead time is usually the time from order placement to receipt of the goods, manufacturing lead time refers to the total time span to manufacture a part (it includes: order preparation, queue time, setup and runtime, move, etc. through to shipment). Though when discussing lead time in value stream mapping of manufacturing processes, we are specifically referring to the TPCT (throughput time in your operations for raw/purchased materisl to pass through to the customer).

Value Stream Mapping in Low-Volume Manufacturing

Value stream mapping was originally set up for high- and medium-volume plants, although it can certainly be applied in low-volume areas. The following strategies are recommended for using value stream maps in low-volume departments or businesses:

- Base the value streams on *product families*, a group of products that pass through similar processing steps or common machines (learn about this in *Creating Mixed Model Value Streams*[1]).
- Base the value stream map on high-running parts.

---

1. Kevin J. Duggan, *Creating Mixed Model Value Streams*. Productivity Press, 2002.

- Complete a general value stream map for the basic processes you have, and then complete a few TPCT lines for some of the higher volume parts.
- Individual value stream maps for each high-volume part number, that is, your runners (assuming each runner follows a different path or uses different materials).
- Individual maps for critical components (or subassemblies).

This book assumes you have some basic value stream mapping knowledge and does not include lengthy explanations of individual terms, concepts, or symbols, although a few of the key symbols are shown in Figure 7-2. For further information, read *Learning to See*.[2]

Figure 7-3 shows a value stream map developed for a low-volume plant, but note that the map follows one of the plant's higher-volume part numbers. Everything in black is the flow of material; everything in gray is the flow of information; and the kaizen bursts shown with the blitz ⟨Blitz⟩ indicate ideas that were added while the map was being created.

You can see that the longest path (which happens to also have the highest cost for inventories) is 64.6 days of non-value-added time and 170 minutes of value-added time (or 0.6% of the time the part is being worked on), a typical result in many industries. We will follow this example through to the future state and then address some issues that arise when mapping in low volume.

When using this method, make sure not to forget the step of changing all inventory measurements into a currency figure (in this case, euros) so that you do not begin working on the flow with the longest total product cycle time without regard to where the biggest potential savings are.

One symbol seldom used in high-volume plants (and, therefore, not covered in some value stream mapping books), is the symbol for shared processes. This symbol, shown in Figure 7-4, is especially important in low-volume operations, because you often have a process/machine that is shared among different products.

In this case, it is helpful to show the percentage of capacity utilized by the value stream you are mapping, as well as the total current percentage the process is utilized by all products (refer to Figure 7-3, where this is demonstrated in CNC #45 & Honing). Filling in these percentages helps to clarify if you have a bottleneck process, for example, if your total utilization is at 90 percent or more (refer to chapter 5). This shared process might even be utilized for many parts or value streams; in other words, it is not dedicated to a particular value stream and will present a management challenge, so visual manage-

---

2. Rother and Shook, *Learning to See*. Lean Enterprise Institute, 1998.

Partial List of Value Stream Symbols

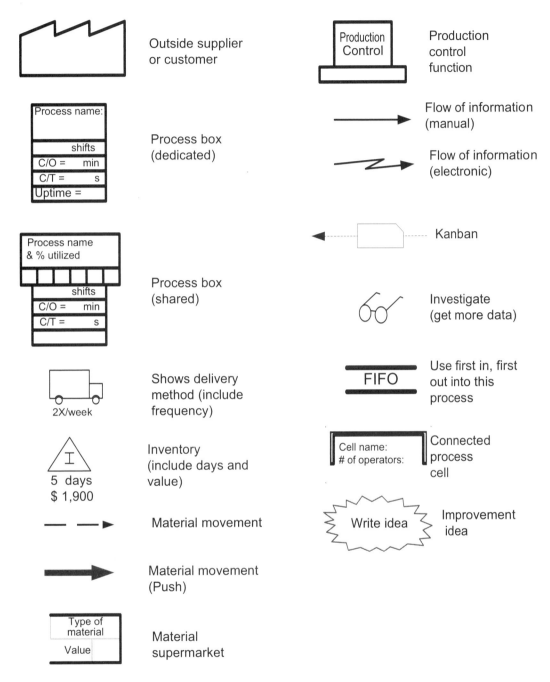

Figure 7-2. Some common symbols used in value stream mapping.

ment at the shared processes is critical to understanding its status. Keep in mind that the solid lines showing the flow of information demonstrate opportunities for improvement in your office processes. "Office Department" and "Office Process" kaizen, or the implementing of a pull system, are some of the methods that can be utilized to make improvements in the flow of information.

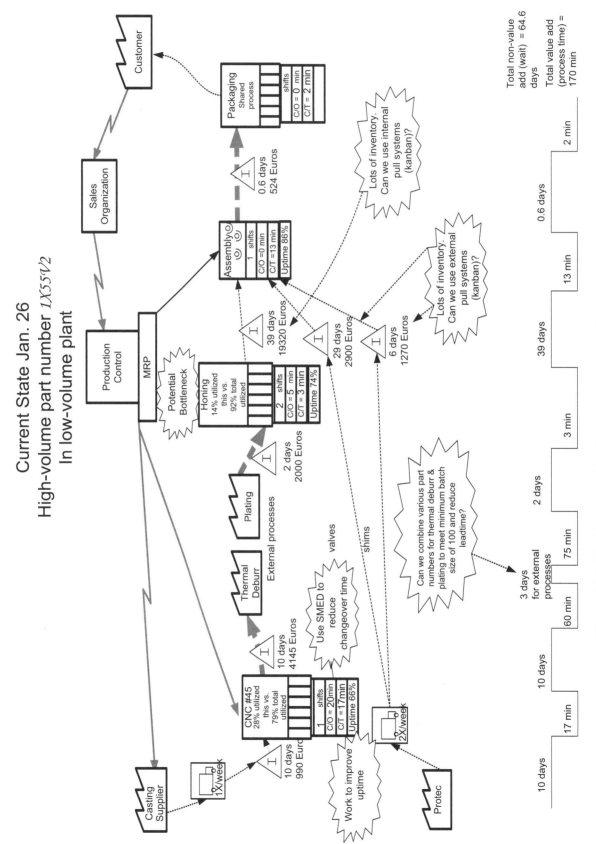

Current State Jan. 26
High-volume part number *1X55V2*
In low-volume plant

Customer

Sales Organization

Production Control

MRP

Packaging
Shared process

shifts	
C/O = 0 min	
C/T = 2 min	

I 0.6 days 524 Euros

Assembly

1 shifts	
C/O = 0 min	
C/T = 13 min	
Uptime 86%	

I 39 days 19320 Euros

I 29 days 2900 Euros

I 6 days 1270 Euros

Lots of inventory. Can we use internal pull systems (kanban)?

Lots of inventory. Can we use external pull systems (kanban)?

Potential Bottleneck

Honing
14% utilized this vs. 92% total utilized

2 shifts	
C/O = 5 min	
C/T = 3 min	
Uptime 74%	

I 2 days 2000 Euros

Plating

Thermal Deburr

External processes

valves

shims

Can we combine various part numbers for thermal deburr & plating to meet minimum batch size of 100 and reduce leadtime?

Use SMED to reduce changeover time

I 10 days 4145 Euros

CNC #45
28% utilized this vs. 79% total utilized

1 shifts	
C/O = 20min	
C/T =17min	
Uptime 66%	

Work to improve uptime

I 10 days 990 Euro

1X/week

Casting Supplier

2X/week

Protec

Total non-value add (wait) = 64.6 days

Total value add (process time) = 170 min

10 days	17 min	10 days	60 min	75 min	2 days	3 min	39 days	13 min	0.6 days	2 min

3 days for external processes

Figure 7-3. Simple example of a current state value stream map.

102

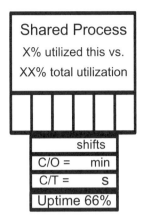

Figure 7-4. Shared process symbol.

Figure 7-5 lists five points you should review before making a future state map. These should help in generating kaizen ideas.

1	**Takt time or day by hour**	Ensure processes are either managed with takt time or day by the hour, whichever is appropriate.
2	**Flow of material**	Move toward smaller batches & one piece flow.
3	**FIFO**	First in, First out for purchased & manufactured parts.
4	**Pull**	Ensure systems (kanban) to replenish usage of high-volume manufactured & purchased parts are utilized.
5	**Single point scheduling**	Schedule at only one process and all other processes are pulled or pushed from this point. Normally push and then flow.

Figure 7-5. Some items to be evaluated for the future state value stream.

For our example, we might draw the conclusions listed in Figure 7-6 about the map shown in Figure 7-3 and add a few more improvement ideas.

IDEAS FOR JAN 26 CURRENT STATE OF PART 1X55V2		
1	**Takt time or day by hour**	Due to shared processes, day by hour should be used instead of takt time. Needs to be implemented at machining, honing and assembly.
2	**Flow of material**	Assembly uses build to order (in smaller batches). Ask customers to separate large orders into split delivery dates, so batching can be avoided.
3	**FIFO**	Review all inventories for systems to ensure FIFO. Use FIFO boards instead of day-by-hour boards where appropriate.
4	**Pull**	Implement internal & supplier kanban, also combined kanban & work order board should be utilized.
5	**Single point scheduling**	Can start pull system to casting supplier & kanban system in machining & only schedule at assembly.

Figure 7-6. Example of five evaluated points from value stream in Figure 7-3.

The ninety-day plan for the future state might look like Figure 7-7, which is a simplified example of value stream mapping for a single part number for a company that decided it could use separate value stream maps for each high-volume part number. Notice that pull systems and supermarkets are planned to reduce the time materials wait in inventory, though on low-volume part numbers you would instead push at the first step and then flow. When you look at the TPCT line at the bottom of Figure 7-7, you see that all the initial improvements focus on the non-value-added times. This is typical as a first step.

Future state value stream mapping for high-mix, low-volume environments demands that attention be focused on a set of characteristics that actually represent the basic differences between high-volume and low-volume plants. A short list of these unique features follows:

- Shared processes

- Imbalance between processes

- Only partially utilized processes

- Infrequent orders

- Large order size variations

- The inability to calculate and plan based on takt time

- Large variation in components/purchased parts used in various products

It would be difficult to discuss all the ways these issues could be handled; for some, there seem to be no viable method to utilize in connection with value stream mapping. Some of the following suggestions, however, should help you develop a good future state in high mix, low volume.

- Put in pull systems (internal or supplier kanban) wherever possible, starting with the most expensive inventories. *Note:* Often a hybrid pull/push system is required for internal kanban in high-mix, low-volume plants. This means that the parts you decide qualify for kanban cannot necessarily pull through each process, because that would require a small amount of inventory between each step. Therefore, you will normally pull between the point of use (consumption) and the first process, and push through the steps in-between, requiring only some inventory prior to the point of consumption. Chapter 4 discusses the two visual systems involved, a combined day-by-hour board with a FIFO board. Chapter 8 discusses how to set up the kanban.

- Work with customers to allow large quantity orders to have split delivery dates. This will allow you to work closer to one-piece flow and should also benefit the customer, especially if the client company is further processing the parts (the company will not be able to use all parts immediately, so its inventory will be reduced).

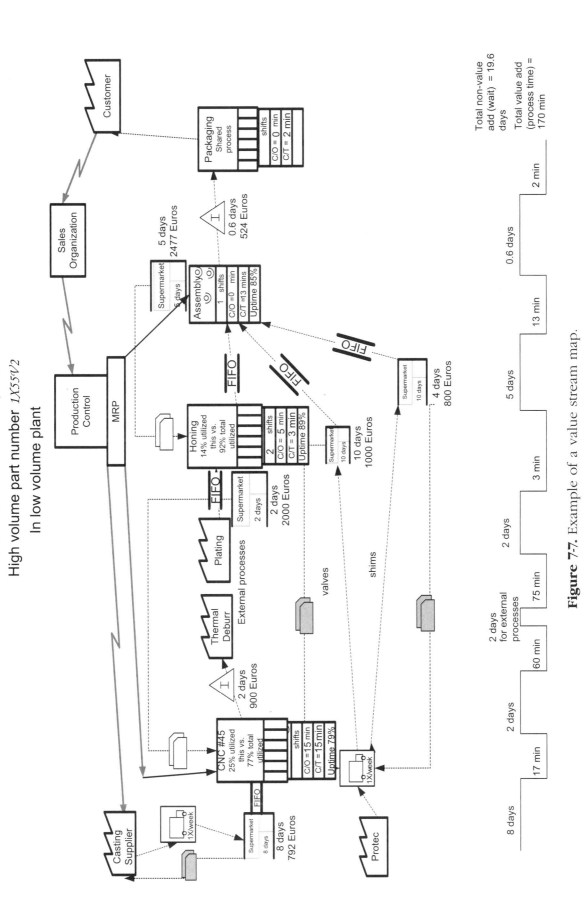

Figure 7-7. Example of a value stream map.

- Focus on long changeover time, specifically improving the time required to adjust the machine on repeating parts.

Summary of Key Points

- Value stream mapping shows your flow of material and information and allows you to identify opportunities for improvement by using certain symbols that represent nonlean practices.

- In high-mix, low-volume companies, you need to decide whether to value stream map based on product families, high-running parts, common processes, and so on.

- Shared processes are common in low-volume plants; include the capacity this value stream utilizes and the total capacity utilized so you can understand all options for improvements.

- After creating the map, review the five evaluation points to help generate kaizen ideas.

- Your future state map should include the improvements you believe are reasonable to target in the near future, for example, during the next three months.

- Managing by value streams instead of functional departments (such as press shop, machining, assembly, and so on) has many advantages that are discussed throughout this book.

8

Becoming Aware of Your Inventory and Using Pull Systems

You always want to be aware of the composition and cost of your inventory. Different businesses have different inventory structures divided among raw materials, purchased parts, work-in-process, and finished goods (see Figure 8-1). In this chapter, we focus on methods to reduce raw materials, purchased parts, work-in-process and any finished goods inventory.

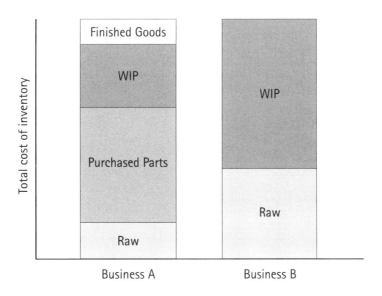

Figure 8-1. Different businesses have different types of inventories.

Inventory Awareness and MRP

MRP (material requirements planning) is a just-in-time tool that helps materials arrive just as they are required. It globally plans for capacity and human resources, but the users of the system tend to get nervous and typically build in extra lead time and safety stock. This makes them feel comfortable that there will not be a shortage of materials or capacity. If you use an MRP system to plan your business and manage your purchases, do *not* assume you have your inventory under control. MRP is the best way to plan if your forecasts are always accurate; but if your forecasts change (or instead you build to order), there is a better method that involves having MRP manage your low-volume parts, while your higher-volume repeating parts (your runners) can be managed by a pull system (usually a kanban system). I call this hybrid solution combining kanban and MRP.

Note: With this combined system it is still possible to procure all materials and print work orders for all work within the MRP system, even for those parts on pull/kanban, if this is necessary. In this case, kanban will authorize production and MRP will procure materials and track costs.

There is a good exercise that 1) allows you see whether there is opportunity within your MRP, and 2) demonstrates whether you have reasonable lead times and minimum order quantities from your suppliers. To start, have your purchasing department put together the information for your major purchased materials in a table like the one shown in Figure 8-2.

The current minimum order size and lead time should be taken from the MRP system. First, list your inventory value from highest to lowest. Then begin contacting the suppliers with the highest inventory values and:

1. Clarify that you have the correct minimum order size and lead time for each part number from that supplier.

2. See whether suppliers will agree to reduce either without a cost increase.

You may be surprised how often the data in an MRP system is incorrect. Perhaps suppliers have already improved their processes and are working in smaller batch sizes with shorter lead times. Or someone may have put in a longer time because he or she felt it would create a safety stock or that it would solve some of the problems with a particular supplier. You may also notice current inventory levels that exceed the minimum order (such as part number 24465 in Figure 8-2), meaning that someone overordered. In this case, try to understand whether this was done accidentally or for a reason.

Completing this table and gathering information is the first step to take with your purchased materials. You can then look at removing your higher-usage parts from the MRP and putting them on a pull system. Most low-volume plants (except in job shops) tend to have some standard parts that represent a significant percentage of their volume. Thus, they might not follow the 80/20 rule, where 20 percent of the part numbers represent 80 percent of

Supplier	Part number	Part cost	Current inventory	Current inventory value	Average monthly usage	Current minimum order size (pieces)	New minimum order size (pieces)	Current lead time (days)	New lead time (days)	Comments
	47-443	$113.54	5	$567.70	2	5		20		*Looking into these part numbers to reduce order qty. & lead time*
	24465	$9.10	45	$409.50	4	12	12	10	5	
Precision Industries	34510	$39.87	9	$358.83	1	4		20		*Looking into these part numbers to reduce order qty. & lead time*
	90-4451	$18.25	14	$255.50	10	1		3		
A-1 Bearings	144532	$24.98	10	$249.80	4	8	4	10	5	*Currently deliver 1X/week. lead time wrong in computer*

Figure 8-2. Determining whether there are opportunities in your MRP system.

the volume (see Figure 8-3) though certain parts are considered "more standard" than others.

Using Different Methods for Runners, Repeaters, and Strangers

Inventory awareness is facilitated when you classify your part numbers and use an appropriate management system for each. Consider first whether your part numbers are runners, repeaters, or strangers:

- **Runners** are the parts you make most often.

- **Repeaters** are ordered periodically (monthly or quarterly).

- **Strangers** are rarely (if ever) repeat orders.

You should not plan for all these parts in the same way. Runners and some repeaters are perfect candidates for a kanban pull system (see the "Kanban Defined" section below for details on kanban systems), while less-frequent repeaters and strangers are better managed as build to order parts through MRP.

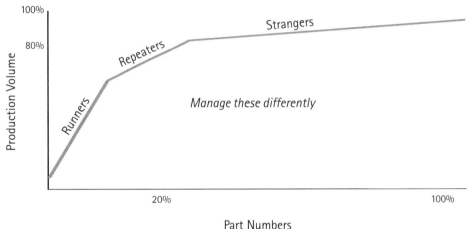

Figure 8-3. Typical breakdown of runners, repeaters, strangers.

Combining Kanban and MRP

As the discussion above suggests, MRP and kanban can work well together. (How to calculate and set up this combination system is explained in the "Calculating the Number of Kanbans" section later in this chapter.) After first setting up kanban within your plant, you can then look at expanding it externally to suppliers and finally to customers (if your business is suited to having any finished or semi-finished parts in stock).

Note: In the case of poorly performing or high-risk suppliers, you may decide on a strategy of purchasing in advance or purchasing the entire quantity at one time, thereby reducing the risk and increasing your inventory. This approach, however, should be periodically reviewed for other options.

Shortening Lead Time

On the shop floor, pull systems can help you to reduce lead time and reduce your inventory (your WIP). The reduced lead time comes mainly from the following:

- Smaller batch sizes (with pull systems), allowing faster and more accurate responses to the customer order

- As a result of producing what the customer is consuming, having the right parts (instead of working to a forecast that might be inaccurate, then producing the wrong parts, and unnecessarily increasing lead times)

Other benefits derived from pull systems are as follows:

- Less capital is tied up in inventory.

- Less inventory means less scrap during model changes.

- Less waste (correction, overproduction, motion, material movement, waiting, and overprocessing) hidden by inventory.

Kanban Defined

Kanban is a Japanese word meaning "visible record" though it is basically used as a signaling system; it is sized to hold what the customer needs and uses. It is based on consumption, using maximum and minimum levels. Kanban is a pull system rather than a *push system*, which is based on forecasted future needs. Physically, kanban usually takes the form of a card, which signals that a certain quantity of material consumed and should be replaced. There are two categories of kanbans:

- **Production instruction kanban:** When sent back to the originating process, this type of kanban authorizes that process to produce something in the amount or quantity noted on the card.

- **Parts withdrawal kanban:** This card (or signal, e-mail, or fax if it moves between separate physical locations) authorizes the receiving location to replace material that has been consumed. This type of kanban is frequently used between an external supplier and a customer.

There are three areas in your plant where you may find it advantageous to use kanban.

- **Internal kanban:** This is normally used within your manufacturing processes, moving from the location where a part is utilized for a customer order back to the first process step. The kanban is pushed through intermediate steps, because pure pull would require too much inventory in a high-mix environment. An internal kanban reduces work-in-process (WIP).

- **Supplier kanban:** This is for high-volume purchased parts and raw materials. A supplier kanban reduces raw materials and purchased part inventories.
- **Finished goods kanban:** This is for high-volume finished products (or in some cases, semi-finished products). A finished good kanban will reduce finished goods inventory.

Note: A word of caution: If you have a process at or near capacity (that is, your current bottleneck), do not try to install kanban until you have a workable option to build a small inventory. This inventory is required for a pull system and is usually difficult to build up if you are already at the limits of your capacity.

Getting Started with Kanbans

When introducing kanban, always start with an internal kanban, one that moves between two processes within your production area. Taking this approach allows you to gain experience before starting kanban with your suppliers or customers, where there are more variables outside of your control. Moreover, be aware of certain risks associated with kanban: Loss of cards and operators not being trained on how to use the system are the most common. To minimize these risks, you need to put in place an audit system for the cards and standardized work and training for operators who will be using them. You should never initiate supplier kanban until these measures are in place.

More or less the same method used to calculate internal kanban levels can be applied to supplier and finished goods kanban; the small differences in the calculation method are discussed later in this section. (Keep in mind, however, that finished goods kanban is rarely used in a low-volume plant, because it is rarely practical to stock some of each finished part number).

The following process is normally used to calculate the kanban level at the first process step only. If there are intermediate processes through which the part is routed, the part should be pushed through these intermediate steps by using a FIFO board (where the finished part is pushed into the FIFO lane of the next process and then noted on the FIFO board so it can be scheduled), as discussed in chapter 4. This hybrid pull/push system is used in high-mix plants because it is not practical to pull between each process step, as this would require inventories at each point for each of the part numbers. (If material needs to be separately prepared for the first step, the kanban should be set up at the first machine; from there, a simple signal is sent to get the material ready. Normally, the material can be quickly prepared when the schedule for the following twenty-four hours is determined, and there is ample time to collect or cut the material, assuming it is in stock.) Almost all methods (and equations) to calculate kanban levels take into account the following four conditions:

- Time to replenish the stock
- Customer variation
- Manufacturing variation (including quality problems and material shortages)
- Emergency stock

You need a quantity of kanban to cover each of these areas. A certain amount of your kanban cards will wait in inventory, while other cards are waiting on the board for replenishment. The amount in inventory is based on 1) how quickly and economically you can change over, 2) the lead time through your system, 3) the variation from the customer, and 4) the variation in your manufacturing processes. The smaller each of these is, the fewer kanban cards, and therefore, fewer parts that are required in inventory.

First, choose some internally manufactured parts that go through more than one process in your plant and are considered runners. To decide which of those parts are suitable for kanban, sort the parts built in a particular process from highest to lowest usage (use the most recent three to six months of actual consumption; don't use forecasts). Then, from this list, choose the highest usage parts (the runners) you feel show enough stability for kanban. These should be parts for which the customer forecasts a future requirement—definitely not a discontinued part! In general, if you do not have a minimum of one part per week consumed, don't consider the part for kanban. Your decision should also take into account the size of a batch you can produce, the cost of the part, the normal quantity of the customer order, the shelf life, and so on. Whatever you choose, start with a small number of parts from one production process. From the data presented in Figure 8-4, for example, you might choose any or all of the nine parts shaded in gray as candidates for kanban. You would probably not consider part #1337790, because although the quantity is 41 pieces, it has been ordered only once. Leave that one as a build-to-order part within the MRP system.

Calculating the Number of Kanbans

I have developed a general method to calculate the number of kanban cards required for a part that includes each of the four conditions (time to replenish stock, customer variation, manufacturing variation, and emergency stock) listed above. It is a very safe and conservative method that starts you out with a high level of kanbans so that the system will not fail; as you become confident, you can reduce the level of cards, which in turn, will reduce your inventory. In the explanation, whenever I refer to the "customer," I am referring to the consumer or user of the parts, whether it is the person running the next production process or the final customer.

Part Number	Total parts consumed (Jan. – Apr.)	Number of times part was ordered (Jan. – Apr.)	Average daily usage
1442344	266	7	3.3
1873367	198	5	2.5
2991528	133	8	1.7
1644367	130	4	1.6
2339450	107	3	1.3
1590322	67	6	0.8
3201214	54	2	0.7
7210034	52	4	0.7
1337790	41	1	0.5
4380122	32	4	0.4
2831001	22	2	0.3
1230012	17	2	0.2
4321172	10	1	0.1
2103321	7	1	0.1

Figure 8-4. A method to select which parts qualify for kanban.

It is easiest to perform your kanban calculations in a spreadsheet. Figure 8-5 shows a typical calculation for one part number, 1442344; Row 5, shows the formulas used. If you follow Row 4 (across the middle of the figure), the white boxes are where you fill in data, and the gray boxes are where calculations are performed. You are simply calculating a separate number of kanban cards for each of the four categories: time to replenish stock; customer variation; manufacturing variation; and emergency stock. Add these four together in Column M, and you have the total number of kanban cards required for this part number.

Column B: Daily Usage

Determining the average daily usage in low-volume plants can be difficult. Many parts have a zero consumption level for days or weeks, and then a large batch might be consumed. (Customers purchasing less frequently, but in larger quantities, can be a reflection of your pricing policies or their ordering methods. Rarely do they need all the parts at once, so it might be worthwhile to look into split deliveries for your customers.)

Try to look, at a minimum, at the last two to three months of usage; you can safely disregard any orders that were exceptional or those you do not expect to repeat. Take an average for this data, including all the zero usage days and compare that number to an average *excluding* all the zero usage days. If the difference in these averages is significant—say, one is three or four

PRODUCTION INSTRUCTION KANBAN CALCULATION

column	A	B	C	D	E	F	G	H	I	J	K	L	M	N	O Red	P Yellow	Q Green
row	Part number	Avg. Daily usage (pieces)	Quantity of parts per kanban card (can be the number of parts in box) (pieces)	Minimum kanban for production batch (in) (kanbans)	Time to replenish the stock (days)	Calculation of kanban cards for replenishment time (in kanbans)	Customer variation (in Standard Deviations)	Calculation of kanban cards for customer variation (in kanbans)	Manufacturing variation (input OEE [or uptime] as a whole number)	Calculation of kanban cards for manufacturing variation (in kanbans)	Emergency Stock (days)	Calculation of kanban cards for emergency stock (in kanbans)	Total Kanban Cards Required for this Part (in kanbans)	Maximum possible days of inventory (days)	Calculate number of positions in red (assume red = when 2 days are remaining) (in kanbans)	Calculate number of positions in yellow (assume 2 days or warning in yellow) (in kanbans)	Calculate number of positions in green (the number of remaining positions) (in kanbans)
4	1442344 (small gear)	3.3	6	2	4	3	4	3	85	1	0	0	7	12.7	2	2	3
5	formulas					=ROUNDUP(((E4*B4)/C4),0)		=ROUNDUP(((G4*E4)/C4),0)		=ROUNDUP((((95-I4)/100)*(E4*B4)/C4),0)		=ROUNDUP(((K4*B4)/C4),0)	=IF(D4>=(F4+H4+J4+L4),D4+1,(F4+H4+J4+L4))	=+(M4*C4)/B4	=ROUNDUP((2*B4/C4),0)	=ROUNDUP((2*B4/C4),0)	=M4-O4-P4

Figure 8-5. Internal kanban calculation spreadsheet.

115

times the other—this part may not be suitable for kanban, because you would have to hold inventory for a time, and then all that inventory would all be simultaneously consumed. You can easily get the average in Microsoft Excel by using =AVERAGE(A1:A15), where A1 and A15 are the locations of the first and last data points, respectively.

Column C: Quantity Per Kanban

To determine the number of pieces of this part (and the smaller, the better) that should constitute a kanban card, you must consider the batch size, the box size, and the usage. Most plants find it easiest to start with the batch size or the box size (whichever is smaller). The box size is the easiest to work with, especially if the process that follows this one (as well as your final customer) always consumes in box quantities. If the batch size happens to be large because of long setup times, first try reducing the changeover time using the SMED method (discussed in chapter 5). If the packing quantity is unnecessarily large, look into repackaging in a smaller container.

Column D: Minimum Kanban for Production Batch

The minimum number of kanbans for a production batch is normally decided by the production manager; a smaller number is always better. It is necessary to compare this number with the total number of kanban cards required (which is calculated in column M). If fewer total cards are required than the minimum batch size, you will never have enough cards returned to the machine to authorize production; however, the spreadsheet will check for this and increase the total number of kanban cards, if necessary. Such a situation is very dangerous, however, usually indicating you have such long setup times that you are inclined to produce very large batches. In this case, undertake a changeover reduction (SMED), and then reduce the minimum batch size. This minimum batch size must be a multiple of the quantity per kanban (see the preceding section of this chapter) and must be clearly indicated on the kanban board so that the production operator understands when he or she can start production (kanban boards are discussed later in this chapter).

Column E: Time to Replenish Stock

Time to replenish is the total time from when a kanban card is returned to the process until the parts are manufactured and made available again at the reordering point. This time includes the average time the card is expected to wait (while the process is completing other kanbans and works orders), plus the time required to manufacture the pieces called for on the card and have them available at the process where the kanban board is located.

You will have to take your best guess at how many working days this will be. Consider how busy the process normally is, the processing time, and any additional processes that are necessary (for example, painting, plating, cleaning), before the item is presented to the point of use. Also, if there are frequent quality problems with suppliers or material shortages, you might add in extra time to cover those problems or add time in column K (emergency stock). Do not, however, compensate in both places. The idea is that you need enough inventory (equivalent to kanbans) to cover a customer's requirements during the time you are refilling an order.

Column F: Calculation

This column is where you calculate the number of kanban cards necessary to cover the period of time during which the kanban is being replenished and the customer is still consuming. In Row 4, the "3" signifies three kanban cards, and because each card represents six pieces, this is equivalent to eighteen pieces. Take the number of days you estimate to replenish and multiply this by the average number of pieces consumed each day—you must divide this by the quantity of pieces in a kanban so that the unit comes out in kanbans. As the equation in column F shows, the number is always rounded up. You may end up with a little extra inventory, but this helps ensure that you will always have material available for the customer (or the next process) when you start the new system. Later on, you can reduce the number of cards. (You might wonder why you don't just round up after totaling all the kanbans that are required for this part, but when you're starting out, you want to be conservative, so it is better to round up each individual category.)

Column G: Customer Variation

The best way to determine customer variation is to use the standard deviation of the data (it should be based on the same data that was used to determine the average daily usage in column B). *Standard deviation* is a measure of how far apart the data are from the average of the data (mathematically speaking, it is the square root of the variance), so it represents how a customer varies in consuming the parts. The easiest way to calculate standard deviation is with Microsoft Excel, using the following equation: =STDEV(A1:A15), where A1 and A15 represent the locations of the first and last data points, respectively. You might compare this standard deviation to the STDEV with all the zero usage days removed. If there is a considerable difference, you will be carrying extra inventory to compensate for an irregular usage pattern. (Be sure you understand what factors are driving your customers into infrequent orders with large quantities and investigate ways to reduce this.)

Customer variation is based on historical use and compensates for variation by increasing inventory. If your customers' forecasts differ considerably from their actual requirements in the past, recalculate your kanban level often.

Column H: Calculation

This column is where you calculate the number of kanban cards necessary to compensate for customer variation. Take the standard deviation from column G (because the usage data is usually by the day, the standard deviation represents how many pieces above or below the average the customer has consumed), and then multiply by the number of days it will take to replenish the kanban and divide by the pieces per kanban card so that the units are in kanban cards.

Round up to be safe, being conservative and assuming the worst case: This means assuming that each day, while you are replenishing the kanban, the customer is consuming one standard deviation more than the average usage. It is unlikely this scenario would happen every day during the replenishment time, but at the beginning, making such an assumption helps ensure that you start with enough kanbans, so that the customer will not run out of parts.

Column I: Manufacturing Variation

Enter your OEE here if you have a machine involved in processing these parts; otherwise, enter the uptime for the process. This should be entered as a whole number (that is, if you have 85 percent OEE, you enter 85). You are adding kanban cards (or inventory) to make up for deficiencies in your manufacturing processes that would prevent a customer from getting parts. (*OEE is the overall equipment effectiveness*, which equals Availability × Performance × Quality and is discussed in more detail in chapter 10).

Column J: Calculation

This column is where you calculate the number of kanban cards necessary to cover the manufacturing variation. Experience has shown that if you have more than a 95 percent OEE or uptime, it is not necessary to add kanbans (or inventory) to buffer against the rare chance that you might have a problem. In the equation presented, if you enter a number above 95, you will come up with a negative number of kanban cards (and therefore, you should disregard it).

You can see in the equation that you convert an OEE (from column I) of anything less than 95 percent into a percentage, then multiply by the number of days to replenish, and then multiply by the average daily usage. This number is then divided by the pieces per kanban and is rounded up. You are assuming that every day, during the replenishment cycle, the machine is operating at the OEE you specified, although it is possible it might perform above or below that number.

Column K: Emergency Stock

Keeping *emergency stock* means adding some extra kanban (inventory) to cover for any other unforeseen problems in your business (other than those related to replenishment, customer variation, and manufacturing variation).

The number you use here is based on your experience in the business and your comfort level in working with kanban. In the example presented in Figure 8-5, the managers felt there was no need to add any extra days' worth of kanbans. I find that about half the companies I work with do not add any emergency stock, while the others add one to two days' worth. If you decide to add emergency stock, think in terms of how many extra days of inventory you want available to compensate for these potential disruptions (the input is always in "days").

Column L: Calculation

This column is where you calculate the number of kanban cards necessary for any emergency stock deemed necessary. The equation simply takes the number of days you entered into column K, multiplies this by the average daily usage of the customer, and then divides the result by the quantity of pieces in a kanban, so that the units are in kanban cards. Round up to be safe.

Column M: Calculation of Total Kanban Cards

This column is where you calculate the total number of kanban cards you need to print. This is done by adding the calculated number of cards used for the following:

replenishment stock + customer variation + manufacturing variation + any emergency stock

This number will be the total number of cards you make and put into circulation, and the number of hooks (spaces) you put on the kanban board. Keep in mind that this number does not represent the *normal* inventory level. It represents the *maximum* inventory that is possible if the customer is consuming slowly (or stops consuming) or if manufacturing is replenishing quickly.

This number might be incorrect if it is smaller or equal to the minimum kanban for production batch in column D. Therefore, the spreadsheet contains an *if statement* (if something is true, something else will happen) to increase the total level of kanban cards by one card over the minimum batch size; otherwise you would run out of material before starting production.

Column N: Calculation

This column calculates the maximum possible days of inventory you would have on hand, assuming all kanban cards have been manufactured and are waiting on the shelf. (In real-life conditions, I find that normally half or less of the kanban cards are in inventory, and the other half are circulating to the process or waiting on the board to be filled.) You calculate this number by taking the total number of kanban cards required for this part, multiplying this number by the pieces in a box, and dividing by the average daily usage.

It is included only so you have a feel for the worst case scenario regarding inventory.

Columns O through Q: Red/Yellow/Green Levels

In these columns, you perform some calculations to help with visual management on the kanban board. Here you calculate how many of the total kanban cards would constitute operating in a red, yellow, or green range.

- Green is the normal (and comfortable) operating range; when your cards are in this range, your performance is typical and no immediate action is required.

- Yellow is a warning; you are running low on inventory and quick action is advisable.

- Red indicates you have reached the critical zone and are now in danger of running out of parts to supply to your customer.

Remember that a card on the board represents an empty space in your inventory, so the board is basically a reverse image of your stock. An empty kanban board means the stock is full, and a full kanban board means you have nothing in stock. A kanban card typically stays with inventory until the inventory is consumed; the card is then sent back to the board and placed on the hooks from left to right, see Figure 8-6, also reproduced in color on page 23.

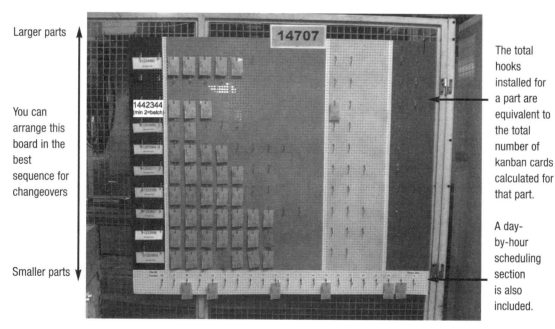

Figure 8-6. Kanban board (related to the calculation in Figure 8-5).

- **Column O—red level:** To calculate the number of kanbans in the red zone, assume management wants to know when you have only two days left in inventory. Normally, it takes four days to replenish the stock, but in an emergency, you could have the parts ready for the customer in two days. Multiply "2" by the average daily consumption and divide by the number of pieces listed on a kanban card. Then round up to ensure you have more than two days remaining.

- **Column P—yellow level:** To calculate the number of cards in the yellow zone, assume management wants a warning when you are two days shy of reaching the red zone. Management feels this is adequate time for production to react. Multiply "2" by the average daily consumption and divide by the number of pieces in a kanban card. Again you round up; otherwise, you have less than a two-day warning.

- **Column Q—green level:** The remaining cards for the part (those not in the red or yellow zones) are in the green zone. Take the total number of kanban cards required for this part from column M, subtract the number used in the red zone (column O), and then subtract the number used in the yellow zone (column P).

Using a Kanban Board

In the kanban board shown in Figure 8-6, all production parts are put on kanban; that is, all parts are runners. Although this rarely occurs in low-volume plants, it can happen when a machine is supplying other internal manufacturing processes. (Note that this board is different from the combined kanban and work-order board shown on page 20, where the process also produces parts not qualified for kanban and are scheduled only when requested by printing a separate work order). Part #144234 (for which the calculations were completed in the spreadsheet), is displayed in the third row on the board. You see there are three hooks in green, two in yellow, and two in red: All seven kanban cards in circulation have a corresponding hook. As parts are consumed, the corresponding kanban card is removed from the box and returned to the board. It is placed on the board from left to right, filling first the green, then the yellow, and finally the red hooks. As the parts are replenished, the cards are removed from right to left.

The board in the figure shows four of the seven cards, signifying that the other three are in inventory or in the process of being returned to the board. Once you have reached the yellow zone, you should begin production as soon as possible, because the inventory level has become critical (there are less than four days of inventory remaining).

Never forget that the image you see on the board is the inverse of your inventory level and dictates what should be produced. An empty hook means you have that kanban (or a box) of material in inventory, while a card on the board signifies that you have an empty space in inventory. Manufacturing's goal is to keep the cards out of red and yellow and work toward filling all the cards (although this rarely happens). This continuously updated visual of your inventory level allows everyone to understand how many parts are usually in inventory and encourages suggestions to adjust this level up or down.

If a machine or process has an optimum sequence in which to perform the changeovers (such as, minimizing changeover time by first running parts with large-diameter holes and gradually changing to small-diameter holes), you can organize the parts on the board in this sequence (see Figure 8-6, which shows changing from larger to smaller parts), and then the planner and team leader can plan the kanbans requiring replenishment (in the white area of the board) according to this sequence. Also, as noted on the board, for part #144234, a minimum of two cards are required to begin production; in other words, the minimum batch size is 12 parts (2 kanbans × 6 parts/kanban).

There are several advantages to using kanban boards. Everyone in the production area understands the current inventory levels and knows which parts are most critical. Thus, the decision about which parts should be produced next is not made in the office, using MRP (at cost), but is made on the shop floor, with the team leaders' involvement. An easy set of guidelines, based on red/yellow/green codes, indicates priorities, and work can be scheduled for the next 24 hours on the lower section (white area) of the board.

Utilizing the Kanban Card

Each kanban card normally contains the following information on the front side (see Figure 8-7).

- Part description
- Part number
- Production process which indicates the kanban board the card is returned to (when you have multiple boards in the plant)
- Quantity of parts in each box (kanban size)

Kanban Card	Small Gear
Part Number	**144234**
Customer's Part Num.	9100540032
Production Process	Machine # 313
Quantity in box (card)	6
Next Process	Deburr (Thermal)
Production Time	1.5 hours
Responsible planner	Jim Hood X433
Card Number	2 of 7

Figure 8-7. Front side of kanban card.

- Name of the next process or the storage location of the finished part
- Manufacturing time to complete production for entire quantity of pieces on card
- Responsible planner/buyer and contact information

- Kanban card number (sequential card number such as 1 of 7, 2 of 7, 3 of 7, and so on)

- Supplier name (if applicable)

- Color coding to help with visualization (that is, material type, part type, product type)

The manufacturing time (required to complete production for the entire quantity of pieces on the card) is placed on the card so each kanban can be scheduled directly on the board. The responsible planner is listed in case the card is damaged or there is some other problem. The card number (2 of 7) is placed on the card so that periodic audits can be completed to ensure all cards are accounted for (lost cards can be dangerous, as production may assume the inventory level is okay when, in fact, it is low).

The back side of the card (see Figure 8-8) contains routing information for additional processes (if you are pushing this part through intermediate processes). In other words, use the backside of the card when you have a kanban part that has further operations. In low-volume manufacturing, it is unlikely you will set up a pull system between each process, because this would require inventory at each step; instead, you push the kanban part through all the intermediate processes, which is why the routing information is required. When the parts are moved to the remaining processes, they should be placed in the FIFO lane, and the FIFO board is updated, as discussed in chapter 4. Sometimes, you will be prioritizing a process between three incoming sources of work: kanbans, work orders, and the FIFO board.

In Figure 8-8, the back side of the card shows the next three processes to which these parts are pushed. Assembly is the last point to which the part is pushed; when the part is consumed at assembly, the kanban card is returned to the board (at machine #313, as noted in Figure 8-7) and becomes a signal to reorder this part number.

Routing	
	Process
1. Deburr (Thermal)	Internal deburring
2. Alodine	Internal plating department
3. Assembly	Assy. Cell 12B

Figure 8-8. Back side of kanban card.

The card will travel with the part through its entire route and will only be pulled and returned to the board when all the parts in the kanban are consumed at the last process noted in the route. If the material is leaving your plant, it is best not to let the card travel externally with the material (it may get lost). With a parts withdrawal kanban for a purchased part, after a box of material is used, the card should be given to the person responsible to e-mail or fax the order to the supplier. While waiting for the replenishment material to arrive, the card can be placed in the receiving area (usually hung on a wall calendar on the date the material is expected to arrive). When the material arrives, the card is put with the material in the stock location. A finished goods part (going directly to the final customer) calls for a production instruction kanban. When the material is shipped, the card is returned to the kanban board at the first production process and is prioritized accordingly.

The First Few Weeks of Kanban

After printing all the kanban cards, you may find that most end up on the board, as you currently have little in inventory. If this is the case, your board will indicate a lot of priorities in the yellow and red zones. It is advisable to allow some time to absorb this new work instead of immediately scheduling overtime or increasing capacity. On the other hand, if you have a lot of parts in inventory, you may need to idle production for a period of time until enough inventory is consumed and cards begin returning to the board.

If you require work orders to manufacture, preprint a few work orders for the parts you put on kanban (usually the work order quantity is equivalent to the "quantity on card" of the kanban). These preprinted work orders are normally placed near the kanban board so that the operator can take the work order when he or she begins work on the kanban. The work orders are not assigned a date, because you do not know when production will begin, but the W/O number provides the authorization to begin working, procures the materials necessary and allows any required tracking of costs or labor.

Short Lead Time Equals Small Inventories

Most value stream maps show that almost all time spent in manufacturing is spent waiting. Normally, a first draft value stream map will show about 99 percent of the time as non-value-added (usually waiting), with 1 percent or less of value-added time, thus transforming the product. You can have up to four types of inventory in your value stream: raw material, purchased parts, work-in-process (WIP), and finished goods. Each of these is discussed in the following sections.

One of the big advantages to the methods discussed here is that they enable you and everyone else involved in a process to visualize and evaluate your inventory. This approach has a great impact on your organization and supports efforts to reduce inventory. Everyone involved sees the inventory level each day, and this promotes a clear understanding of where it is and why it exists. It also encourages suggestions on how to reduce it. This is a very different approach from that used by traditional business models in which a team from purchasing or production control is assigned to reduce inventory by analyzing it on paper.

Raw Material and Purchased Parts

A large portion of total wait time can be found in the raw material and purchased parts inventory. The two variables that cause large amounts of inventory (and therefore waiting time) in these areas are:

- Large minimum order quantities
- Long lead times from the supplier

If you could purchase one piece at a time (without incurring a high cost per unit for doing so) and always have it the next day, you would probably need little inventory. Although it is unlikely that you can do this, you can and should have your purchasing team focus on finding suppliers with small minimum order quantities and short lead times, even if this means incurring a small price increase (obviously, you need to weigh this against the cost of carrying inventory). To make this work, first map your high-volume products, as discussed in chapter 7, to help you understand for which part number you have large inventories. Once you have created your list of part numbers with large inventories, put together a table like the one shown in Figure 8-2. Finally, work with the suppliers of these parts, or try sourcing to new suppliers, to reduce your minimum order size and lead time.

Another good method to reduce inventory cost is to have a *consignment stock arrangement* with your supplier. In this case, the supplier keeps predetermined amounts of certain materials on site (at your plant), but you pay for these materials only when you use them. This keeps excess material out of your value stream and does not tie up your capital. This arrangement may be difficult for low-volume and job-shop plants, however, as they tend not to use a significant amount of any material and therefore have little leverage over their suppliers to set up consignment stock. But you don't know if you don't ask!

After you have tried consignment stock or reducing minimum order size and shortening lead times, put your higher-volume materials and purchased parts on a supplier kanban (a type of parts withdrawal kanban). This chapter has already explained how to set up internal kanban; from this point, it will describe the process of setting up supplier kanban. The major differences between internal kanban and supplier kanban are as follows.

- **Replenishment time:** This is the time required by the supplier beginning when the parts are consumed and notification is sent until the replenishment parts arrive in your plant and are back in stock available for use. You need to include the time necessary to send the order via fax or e-mail (in many plants this is done once per day, so you need to add at least one day for this).

- **Customer variation:** This amount now becomes your *order variation.* You take the standard deviation (as previously discussed for internal kanban) of your order quantities. If your orders are currently placed infrequently, convert this number to the standard deviation per day.

- **Manufacturing variation:** This number becomes the *supplier's delivery variation.* If the supplier agrees to deliver in five working days, you should look at the times (over the last three months) that the supplier required more than five days. Input the average number of days the supplier's delivery came after five days. If you have no experience with the supplier, you can estimate: base your estimate on how difficult it would be to obtain the part elsewhere, the proximity of the supplier, and your comfort level.

- **Emergency stock:** As with an internal kanban, this number is based on your experience and comfort with a particular supplier and a specific part number. Think in terms of how many days of extra inventory you want to cover for problems. You can include inventory for any anticipated quality problems from your supplier or to cover for any extra scrap you expect when further processing the part.

In Figure 8-9, you see that the same spreadsheet used for internal kanban (Figure 8-5) can be used for supplier kanban, with a few modifications. By setting this up and trying different numbers, you can see what has the most dramatic effect on the total number of kanbans (which represent your inventory level). Most important is the time to replenish stock in column E, because this number has the strongest impact on your kanban level (the shorter this time, the fewer kanbans required and the lower your inventory). To convince a supplier to work with kanban, you might need to point out the advantages of the system to the supplier's organization. The most important selling points are listed below:

- Kanbans are equivalent to a standardized box size and, therefore, equivalent to a standard order quantity (or a standard multiple order quantity).

- You have factored in the supplier's lead time, so rush orders should not be necessary.

- The supplier can keep one or more completed boxes (kanbans) in inventory and have flexibility in scheduling their production.

- The supplier can use kanban parts to level its own workload. It can choose to refill the inventory of kanban parts during slow production periods.

- The supplier can offer short lead times, thus securing more business.

SUPPLIER (PURCHASED PARTS) KANBAN CALCULATION

column / row	A	B	C	D	E	F	G	H	I	J	K	L	M	N	O	P	Q
	Part number	Avg. Daily usage (pieces)	Quantity of parts per kanban card (can be the number of parts in box) (pieces)	Minimum kanban for supplier order (in kanbans)	Time for supplier to replenish the stock (days)	Calculation of kanban cards for replenishment time (in kanbans)	Order variation (in quantity of Standard Deviations/day)	Calculation of kanban cards for your order variation (in kanbans)	Supplier's delivery variation (average days late)	Calculation of kanban cards for supplier's delivery variation (in kanbans)	Emergency Stock (days)	Calculation of kanban cards for emergency stock (in kanbans)	Total Kanban Cards Required for this Part (in kanbans)	Maximum possible days of inventory (days)	Red — Calculate number of positions in red (assume red = when 5 days are remaining) (in kanbans)	Yellow — Calculate number of positions in yellow (assume 5 days or warning in yellow) (in kanbans)	Green — Calculate number of positions in green (the number of remaining positions) (in kanbans)
3	97732882 (Bushing)	11.1	36	2	8	3	2	1	3	1	5	2	7	22.6	2	2	3
4	6449321 (Piston block)	1.1	8	1	8	2	1.1	2	5	1	15	3	8	56.0	1	1	6
5	formulas					=ROUNDUP((E4*B4/C4),0)		=ROUNDUP(((G4*E4)/C4),0)		=ROUNDUP((I4*B4/C4),0)		=ROUNDUP(((K4*B4)/C4),0)	=IF(D4>=(F4+H4+J4+L4),D4+1,(F4+H4+J4+L4))	=+(M4*C4)/B4	=ROUNDUP((5*B4/C4),0)	=ROUNDUP((5*B4/C4),0)	=M4-O4-P4

Figure 8-9. Supplier kanban calculation spreadsheet.

- The supplier can plan production lot sizes based on kanban size, allowing it to manufacture to the most economical batch size.

- You will set up a blanket order, guaranteeing that the supplier receives orders during the specified period (kanban would be the release method for having parts shipped from the blanket purchase order).

Work-in-Process (WIP)

The best way to keep your WIP at a minimum is to use internal kanbans or put in FIFO boards (see chapter 4). The method presented for setting up an internal kanban discussed in this chapter will start you with a high level of kanbans, so it's important to reduce this level as soon as you have some experience. You'll soon be able to judge to what point to reduce your kanban level and/or which variations are causing the need for a higher level.

Because the kanban board (see Figure 8-6) displays the status only at the current time, you might want to keep a history of the board to help judge whether you can reduce the level or need to add to the level of kanban. One approach to this is to mark the status of the board at the same time each day.

Note: The time you choose should be a stable point in the day for the board and the process; for example, not immediately after the team leader from the previous process returns all cards from the previous shift. Keep a running total of when you are in the red/yellow/green zones, as shown in Figure 8-10.

Part 1442344	red:	yellow: II	green: NN IIII

Figure 8-10. Historical tracking of a part number on the kanban board.

In this case, you were mostly in the green zone and in the yellow zone only twice, so you should be able to remove at least one card. If you were frequently in the red zone, you might need to add some cards.

Finished Goods Inventory

Most low-volume plants do not keep an inventory of finished goods, and rarely will a job shop have any finished goods in stock. If possible, keeping some low-risk finished goods on hand can help you level your workload and increase your on-time delivery to your customers. The finished goods can be set up on kanban using the method presented in this chapter. It is recommended that you sort through the parts you sold over the last six months, organizing them from highest quantity to lowest quantity. Then see whether you think any of these parts are stable enough and are purchased in small enough quantities (if not, review why they are purchased infrequently in large quantities) to allow them to be set up on kanban. You use the same calculation method used for internal parts.

Using both MRP and Kanban

At this stage, you can probably see that MRP and kanban can be used together in high-mix, low-volume plants, and that this hybrid solution has many advantages:

- Kanban for your runner parts and some of your repeaters allows the shop floor to balance demand with the available capacity more easily.
- Kanban allows everyone to understand the critical nature of each part number.
- Kanban gives the shop floor the ability and means to schedule and saves the planning department time.
- MRP can be used to plan globally for raw material, capacity, and human resources (as forecasts are still input and work orders are generated for kanban parts).
- MRP still schedules all strangers so that there is no excess inventory and no obsolete parts are produced (actual orders instead of forecasts are input into the MRP).
- Kanban levels are adjusted in line with forecasts.

Combining kanban and MRP can be simplified by automating the process of recalculating kanban levels. Raymond Louis's book *Integrating Kanban with MRP II*,[1] provides a good explanation on how to do this.

Moving Materials within Your Plant

Forklifts are an inefficient way to move materials; they essentially move only pallet-size loads, one pallet at a time, and often return empty. They may also move material when it is available or when required, but because forklifts do not work at any regular intervals, they do not help in establishing a takt or flow within your plant. Forklifts also tend to have poor safety records.

Tuggers, on the other hand, are usually small electric tow vehicles that can tow multiple carts; some tuggers having up to eight carts in tow. Tuggers can pick up and drop off raw materials or finished goods, small or large quantities, and they can make loops, thus never traveling empty. They move everything

---

1. Raymond Louis, *Integrating Kanban with MRP II, Automating a Pull System for Enhanced JIT Inventory Management.* Productivity Press: New York, 1997.

from small to large parts, kanbans, tooling, and paperwork, either from receiving or between processes and departments (see Figure 8-11). They can be set up on hourly routes to move materials, thereby setting a pace or takt for flowing the materials and establishing a rhythm for production. Very creative ways to move large parts can be found either by using some type of roller device or by exchanging an empty cart for a full one (where a hoist is used at the work station to load and unload the carts).

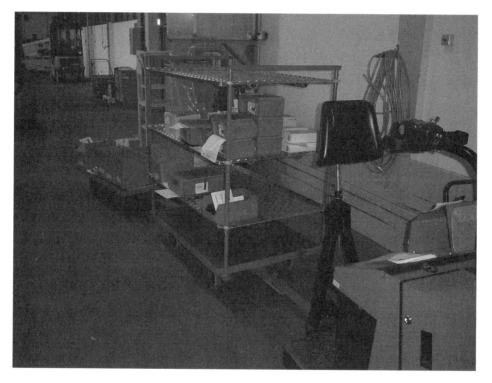

Figure 8-11. Tugger towing two carts.

As Figure 8-12 illustrates, there is a decisive advantage to using a tugger rather than a forklift, even when moving large pallets. Although you may need a forklift on each end to load and unload the tugger, the same movements can be accomplished with three instead of seven people and the process utilizes less equipment. When moving smaller materials, the tugger is even more practical and efficient.

As a rule, it is almost always better to move material in small quantities, rather than filling pallets (which is required when moving with a forklift). The bottom line, then, is to use tuggers instead of forklifts whenever possible. With some creativity, you will find that almost everything can be moved with tuggers. Do not worry about starting with a complete tugger system in your plant; instead, lease one tugger and start with a few simple carts and a simple route. People working in your plant will become creative with what can be moved by

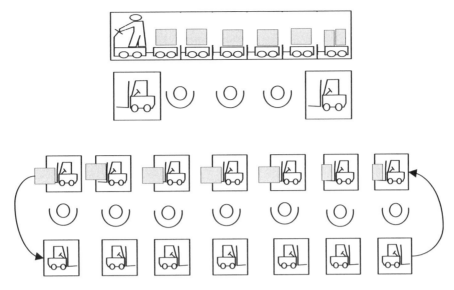

Figure 8-12. Manpower required with a tugger versus with forklifts.

this system, and management can use the tugger's regular interval schedule to assess production and make material flow better.

Summary of Key Points

- Pull systems shorten lead times on the shop floor by:
  - Encouraging smaller batch sizes
  - Indicating what the customer has actually consumed and not encouraging you to potentially build the wrong parts based on incorrect forecasts
- There are two types of kanbans:
  - Production instruction
  - Parts withdrawal
- When calculating the kanban level, it is better to start with a high level so the system will not fail; reduce it as soon as you are comfortable.
- Kanban can be used for:
  - Internal production, helping reduce your WIP and balancing your available capacity
  - Purchased (supplied) parts, helping reduce raw and purchased part inventory levels
  - Finished goods, keeping a low level of finished goods to balance uneven customer demand and more evenly balance your work load
- Visualizing your inventory is the key to reducing it.

- In a high-mix environment, a hybrid pull/push system is required to eliminate the need for multiple points of inventory of many different part numbers.

- Do not forget to establish standardized work (presented in chapter 9) for all operators involved in the handling of kanban cards, and for any office functions affected by the kanban system.

- MRP and kanban can be used together and there are many advantages to combining them.

- Tuggers are more efficient at moving material than forklifts and they create a pace for manufacturing.

9

Making Manpower Improvements

To improve your manpower utilization, this chapter gives you eight techniques that, when applied, reduce the time necessary to complete a task. Some of these methods have already been presented in some form in this book, but this chapter summarizes them and details those that have not been previously discussed. The eight recommended improvements are as follows:

- 5S (workplace organization)
- Standardized work
- Operator balance walls
- Day-by-hour charts
- Cross-trained team members
- Motion kaizen
- Teamwork (with team leaders)
- Andon systems

Some of these methods are somewhat difficult to apply in high-mix production plants and in job shops, so this chapter presents some variations that facilitate application in such environments. Keep the following in mind when implementing any of these techniques: Because they involve changing a working method (and thus creating new work standards), there will initially be a negative effect as operators learn new ways of doing things. Fortunately, the learning curve is usually quick, and any problems associated with it will be temporary.

5S

The *5S concept* of sort, straighten, shine, standardize, and sustain is meant to implement and sustain workplace organization. 5S specifically improves utilization of manpower, because it addresses the fact that considerable time and effort are often wasted looking for and getting tools and materials.

Workplace organization is not only valid on the shop floor but also in the office. Walking to pick up materials or tools is usually non-value-added, and looking for misplaced tools (or tools without standard locations) is *definitely* non-value-added. Therefore, 5S is a good starting point on any shop floor, because it is hard to move ahead with standardization if you are working around the instability and waste of missing or misplaced tools and materials.

Begin 5S whenever you identify time lost because of disorganization, whether during normal production, setups, maintenance, or standard office work. The following five sections provide a brief overview of the steps for 5S; they are usually performed in this sequence.

Sort

To *sort* is to get rid of unnecessary items. Usually, sorting is accomplished by a cross-functional team putting red tags on all items deemed "unnecessary." This normally includes equipment, tooling, materials in the shop, documents, piles of paperwork, and machines in the office. Sorting allows everyone to see clearly the items that have been tagged as unnecessary and express any concerns before these items are discarded.

Straighten

To *straighten* is to organize. This is accomplished by cleaning an area and then finding or creating standard storage places for items that have not been red-tagged. Some ideas that come from the straighten step include creating address systems, using colors to denote locations, using shadow boards (in which an outline of each item is drawn on a board, so that if the item is not hung there, everyone sees that it is missing), putting signboards and labeling in place, marking the floor for flow, changing from closed to open storage systems, organizing by frequency of use, and so on.

Shine

To *shine* is to put in place daily cleaning procedures. You need to decide the following:

- What to clean
- How often to clean it

- What method to use

You also need to prepare the cleaning equipment, do any tool maintenance, and set in place a tracking chart with responsibilities clearly marked.

Standardize

To *standardize* is to maintain a spotless workplace. This step is the most difficult one, because it requires ongoing effort from everyone. You continuously need to remind the team of the following:

- No unnecessary items
- No dirt
- No items out of place

Sustain

To *sustain* is to institute visual controls to maintain cleanliness, usually through an audit procedure that involves a checklist and scoring system. You want a workplace in which problems can be recognized at a glance and management listens to and supports operators frequently, not only during audits (see more in chapter 2). Therefore, this step requires training and discipline.

Standardized Work

Standardized work is the current most efficient working method that produces the best quality product. It changes every time an improvement in the method is found (hence the word "current"). The reason standardized work is important in the context of manpower improvements is that it identifies the most efficient methods and is the baseline for all improvements.

It is difficult to improve a job if the operator performs it in a different way every cycle; the same applies if different operators use different methods. (Keep in mind that when I discuss all operators working to the same standard in low-volume manufacturing, I mean completing the *elements*—the smallest amount of work that should remain together—in the same sequence, not necessarily performing detailed movements in the exact same way.) One working standard is usually written for a single operator's work, although it may be linked to another operator's standardized work, as some tasks require operators to work together.

Standardized changeovers are another form of standardized work, and these are critical in low-volume manufacturing because you perform more changeovers. Using the single minute exchange of dies (SMED) methodology (discussed in chapter 5) is an excellent way to reduce your changeover times, but you need to start with changeover work standards before you can make improvements. Therefore, you should first have standardized work in place for your changeovers as the baseline for making improvements, and then use the SMED methodology to help find opportunities for improvement.

Writing work standards is not about obtaining exact data; instead, it is about observing a job, determining the best sequence in which to complete individual tasks that make up the job, and identifying and implementing improvements. In low-volume plants, you should be concerned with having standards for either the 20 percent of your high-volume part numbers that might account for as much as 80 percent of your production volume, or grouping your work into product families and having a standard that represents the best work sequence for the family of parts. Job shops should have at least a general standardized work sequence for setups, inspections, assemblies, and so on; then they can use day-by-hour (see chapter 4) as a method to ensure an efficient sequence is followed for their wide variety of parts. Depending on the type of product and the type of work performed (for example, machining versus assembly), you may need different formats for the worksheets you use to create work standards. There are many ways you can structure standardized work, but the following list provides a practical template:

- Provide a clear description and show sequence of elements. (These descriptions should not be too detailed, as team leaders will train new operators.)
- Show the key points for each element.
- Show the working time for each element and the total working time (this is necessary to measure improvements); working time should also be compared to takt time, where possible.
- Capture any quality and safety issues.
- Create a management tool for auditing the process to see normal versus abnormal.

Note: Any time you are able to create an assembly cell (that is, physically linked machines or assembly stations where common work elements are performed on similar parts or families of parts), you can and should also utilize standardized work.

There are five steps for creating standardized work:

1. Decide which processes require standardized work (chapter 5 also presents options for which processes require standardized work).
2. Observe the process.
3. Identify the work elements and the most efficient sequence.
4. Measure the element times for manual and machine elements (ten repetitions of each cycle are recommended).

5. Fill out the standard operation sheet, inputting details, as necessary.

A brief description of each step is provided in this chapter. For readers interested in more specific information, there are numerous books on standardized work that are considerably more detailed. The key thing to remember is that you need some stability in a process before you attempt to standardize that process. If you have frequent equipment breakdowns or material shortages, or if the process is not conducive to repeatable human movements, you will need to resolve these issues beforehand.

Deciding Which Processes Require Standardized Work

To decide which processes require standardized work, review the following, and select the approach that is most appropriate for your environment:

- Choose the top 20 percent of high running parts and develop standard work for each type or family of parts (assuming this is a feasible quantity).

- Group parts into product families based on the similarity of manufacturing tasks, and have one work standard per family (use this approach only if one worksheet can represent a family). This is done by completing a product family matrix in which one axis contains the process steps and the other axis the part numbers.

- Separate higher-volume jobs into work elements, and then group similar work elements together, defining a standard method and time for each of these elements. Develop a database (for example, using Microsoft Access) to link a part number to its necessary work elements, so that the operator can access the documents necessary through the database. The database would contain one work standard for each different work element associated with a part number.

- If you do not have the resources or time to undertake any of the previously mentioned methods, develop standardized work as needs are identified. When you have a quality problem because of an incorrect work sequence or because a step was forgotten, write and post the standard. If you find a process being done differently by various operators or if a process is shown to be inefficient, write the standard. If a new tool or piece of equipment is purchased, write a work standard for how to use it. Before you begin standardizing, you will need to develop a documentation format; then, as you identify the processes in need of work standards, you can begin documenting. While this is not the best option, it gets you started.

Note: You also have some options for how you determine standard times. You can use a stopwatch method (as described in the following section) or you can use the Maynard Operation Sequence Technique (commonly known as MOST), which works just as well and may even be easier for low-volume manufacturing. This fast and simple method uses a predetermined motion-time system. There are various methods within MOST, including MiniMOST, BasicMOST, MaxiMOST, and AdminMOST. MaxiMOST is recommended, as it is most suitable for nonrepetitive, low-volume environments with long cycle time operations, whether they are manual or automatic assembly and/or involve machinery. This system is faster and simpler than other similar techniques; it's accurate and consistent; it encourages improvement; and it can be learned in as little as four days. Some lean companies even train their team leaders in creating MaxiMOST standards. Readers interested in these systems can easily find relevant books and courses on the Internet. For simplicity's sake, this book presents only a simplified stopwatch timing method.

Observing the Process Using a Stopwatch

During an observation, begin by using a form with a place to make a sketch of the work area, a section to list the elements, and a section for any problems observed (see Figure 9-1). All these forms should be completed in pencil, as should the standardized worksheet, to facilitate updates.

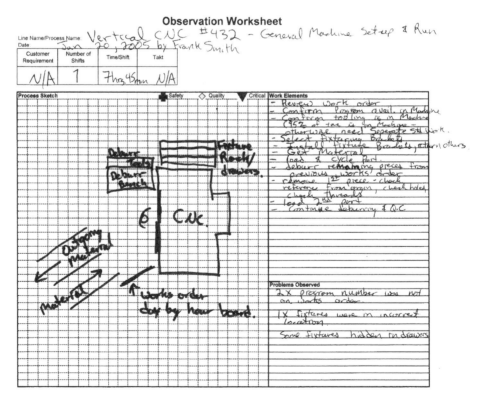

Figure 9-1. Observation worksheet.

Identifying the Work Elements and the Most Efficient Sequence

If one or more operators use different sequences during your observations, you must choose the best sequence for safety, quality, and efficiency. A form like that presented in Figure 9-2 can help put this in order. If the elements are simple and the starting points are obvious, you can skip this sheet and move directly to the time-measurement sheet, like the one shown in Figure 9-3.

You see in this example that most starting points are denoted by the word "touch." You also notice that this particular sheet is being completed for a standard setup on a particular machine, so it includes two other, less frequent, processes (putting correct tooling in the machine and changing fixtures) that require separate work standards.

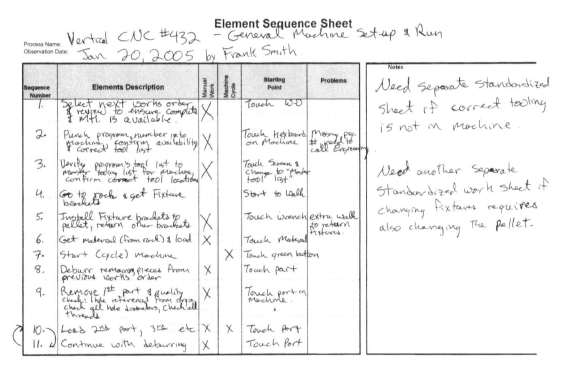

Figure 9-2. Element sequence sheet.

Measuring the Element Times

This step can be difficult in low-volume manufacturing, but the more observations you can make, the more secure your data. Remember that making a video of the process is the quickest and easiest way to get this data. A form like the one shown in Figure 9-3 is recommended, as is using a stopwatch with "lap memory" so you can concentrate on observing the process and write up the data afterward.

Look for the lowest time that repeats. Also time any elements that are not performed in each cycle and determine how often they are performed, so that you can average this time and include it in your observations. These *non-cyclical* elements can be critical in determining your product cost.

Time Measurement Sheet

Line Name/Process Name: Vertical CNC #432 - General Machine Set-up & Run
Date: Jan 21, 2005 by Frank Smith

Part number observed

Sequence number	Element Description	Starting Point	1 (17731)	2 (18614)	3 (23364)	4 (46318)	5 (61779)	6 (54217)	7 (J8367)	8	9	10	Lowest & Most Repeated Element Time	Problems
1.	Select next works order & review & Mtl available	Touch W/O	2'	2.3'	4'	2.5'	1.5'	2.5'	2.2'				2.5'	
2.	Punch in program number & verify prg. & verify tool list	Touch Keyboard	3'	2'	(8')	3.2'	1.8'	(10')	3'				3'	O = missing Prg number
3.	Verify tool list with Master tool list, verify tool locations	Touch Screen	4.2'	4'	6'	3.8'	4.1'	5'	4.2'				4.2'	
4.	Go to rack & get fixture brackets	Start to Walk	3'	3.5'	(7')	2.9'	(8')	2.8'	3.9'				3'	O = fixtures in drawers
5	Install fixture brkts, return others	Touch wrench	10'	12'	17'	9'	10'	13'	9.5'				10'	
6.	Get Material (from rack) & load	Touch Material	2'	2'	3.5'	2.2'	2'	2.4'	2.8'				2'	
7.	Start (cycle) Machine	Touch green button	1'	0.8'	1'	0.8'	1'	1.2'	1'				1'	
	Machine cycle Time	Use avg. cycle for high Runners	13'	17'	22'	14'	15'	12'	11.8'				Avg from 20% high runners 14.8'	
8.	Deburr pieces from previous W/O	Touch Part	6'	9'	13'	8'	6'	5'	6'				6'	
9.	Remove 1st part & Q.C.	Touch Part	12'	8'	14'	8.5'	7'	8'	11'				8'	
10.	Load 2nd part	Touch Part	2'	1.5'	2.5'	1.5'	1.5'	2'	2.2'				1.5'	
11.	Deburr one part (avg. deburr)	Touch Part.	13'	9'	14'	8'	7.5'	8'	9'				8'	

Task ID	Non-Cyclic - Infrequent Work Elements	Starting Point	1	2	3	4	5	6	7	8	9	10	Lowest & Most Repeated Element Time	Problem
	Clean Chips from machine (2X/day)	take broom	8'	–	–	–	–	–	9'				8.5'	

Figure 9-3. Time measurement sheet.

In Figure 9-3, you see that each timing sequence (1–7) is for a different part number (they are obviously all similar in work content, therefore they form a product family). The circles around individual numbers show where the operator had a problem; elements (or rows) with many circles indicate significant problems and require problem solving. You also see that approximately every seven part numbers, you must clean the chips from the machine; this time (and cost) must be averaged into the overall time.

Filling Out a Standardized Operation Sheet

You may have already selected the form(s) to be used in your plant, but it is likely you will need a few forms, depending on the various types of operations you have. Included in this section are a few form templates that you can consider using. Remember that you must first clarify the purpose of the form, as this will determine what information you will be recording.

In Figure 9-4, you have manual work combined with an automatic machine cycle; therefore, you should include a combination table in your form (this should be used only when you have an automatic machine cycle time). Using this format, you can show graphically that you have a forced wait time ⬌ of 8.8 minutes while the machine is cycling (14.8 minutes machine cycle – 6 minute deburr time while machine is running = 8.8 minutes the operator is forced to wait). Note that the walking times have been separated from the manual work times because walking always signals an opportunity for improvement.

Because this document will be used for training, for reminding operators of key points, and for management's auditing the process, other points included here are a drawing to help clarify critical points and sequence, a list of other critical points, and a layout showing where each element is performed (this also helps show where improvements can be made to reduce walking).

Remember that this is the *current* best method, one that presents lots of opportunities: a forced wait time when instead we should rebalance and have the operator do some value-added work; a lot of walking to get the fixtures; and so on. For a case like this, include a combination table.

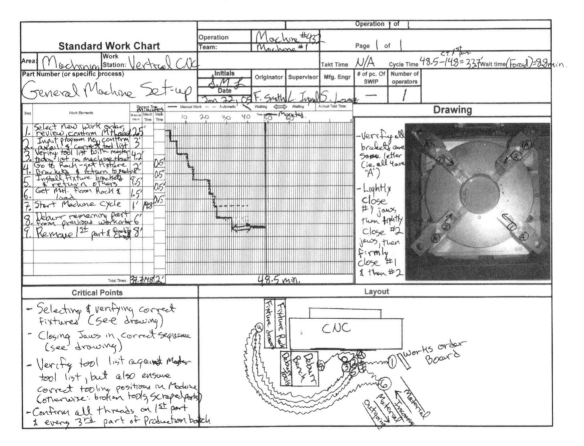

Figure 9-4. Standard work chart.

Figure 9-5 illustrates how a planned maintenance procedure was documented. Other information, such as tools required, safety equipment or concerns, a drawing of the part including critical points, some quality specifications that should be checked by the operator, etc., can also be included on this form. Remember to complete these forms in pencil.

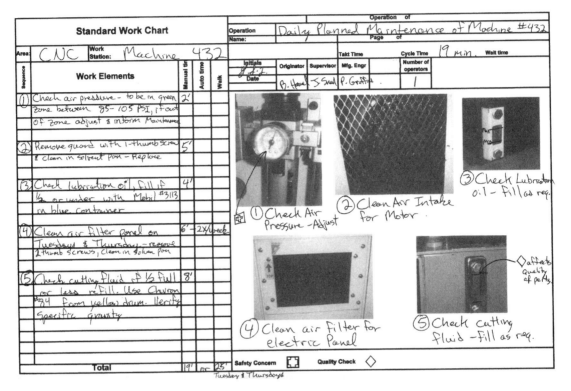

Figure 9-5. Standard work for a planned maintenance procedure.

Office procedures should also have work standards (see Figure 9-6). In the office, you need to record the average time to complete the procedure or the time to process one piece (one order, one drawing, one part, one page, and so on). Flow charts can be helpful, as many procedures have decision points and build in additional work time if additional processes are required.

Operator Balance Wall

The *operator balance wall* is a visual tool that shows the relationship between one operator's work elements and another operator's work elements within a team. It also shows the total workload or balance between each operator and the relationship between the operators' cycle time and the takt time (customer demand). This tool is applicable only where you have dedicated processes, so that takt time is applicable (as discussed in chapter 3).

The *team* that is displayed on one balance wall usually consists of those operators who work together to complete a process/product. For example, if three operators work together to complete an assembly, their standardized work

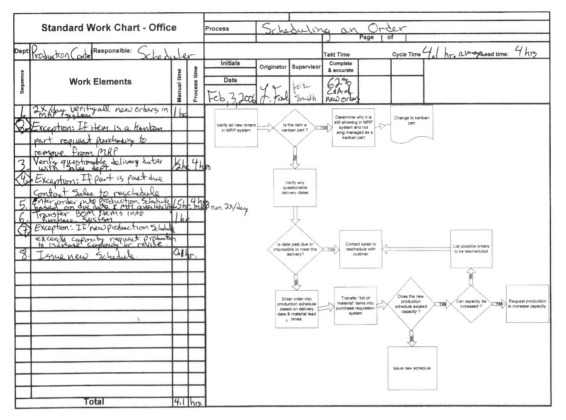

Figure 9-6. Standard work for an office process.

elements are shown together on one balance wall. A separate stacked bar is displayed for each operator. The biggest advantage of the visualization on a balance wall is that it points out opportunities and lets everyone get involved in understanding the process/product and suggesting improvements.

Improving the Balance

In Figure 9-7, reproduced in color on page 24, there are three operators working in an assembly cell with a 30-minute takt time (*takt time* = time available/customer quantity required during the same period). This number is shown by the red line at 30 minutes. The basic information presented on a balance wall is as follows:

- Each operator's *cycle time* (the time required to complete the work elements) compared with the takt time

- The time it takes to complete each individual element and whether it is value-added (in white), non-value-added (in red), or a forced wait (in red stripes)

- How well the work is balanced between the operators

- By moving the red takt-time line when the customer changes the requirements, the wall shows how manpower will be affected.

The wall can be used to display graphically (using colors and symbols) many other considerations for rebalancing as well as any inefficiency. For example, symbols may be used to mark elements that require certain tools (or that should be performed by the same operator), while colors might be used to show which area or orientation of the part is required to perform the element. Critical manufacturing sequences that must be maintained can also be noted, an approach that helps you to keep in mind all factors that are important to individual elements as you contemplate changing the sequence of those elements.

Because you know that red stripe elements are forced wait times (meaning you are paying an operator to wait for a machine cycle or another process to finish), you can probably reduce those through rebalancing. Assuming you are able to remove these, in Figure 9-7 you have about 22 minutes of work with operator #1, 21 minutes of work with operator #2, and 7 minutes of work with operator #3. (22 + 21 + 7 = 50 minutes, or a total of 50 minutes of work within a 30-minute takt time.) You can further assume that this work could be completed by two operators (50 minute total work/30 minutes takt time = 2 operators), if you eliminate the forced waiting time.

Some textbooks encourage balancing the operators to takt time; in other words, load the operator to 100 percent. This author does not recommended using this tactic—it almost never works because there is no time to recover from any problems. Instead, aim for about 80 percent of takt time (in the preceding example, 25 minutes of work in a 30-minute takt time means the operator is 83 percent loaded). Toyota usually balances to 95 percent of takt, but keep in mind that the company has stabilized most problems and has team leaders in place to handle most disturbances. In some plants, "actual takt time" (rather than "pure takt time" as discussed in chapter 4) is shown on the balance wall, which allows managers to see problems and inefficiencies.

You also want to look into reducing some of the time required for the non-value-added elements (red bars), because these normally include walking and picking up materials. You should be able to introduce improvements easily—by relocating the parts so that they are closer to the point of use. (Remember that non-value-added time is something the customer is not necessarily willing to pay for. It does not mean the work is unnecessary, simply that you should try to minimize this time).

Note: One strategy to employ during busy times is to have a separate material handler do some of the walking and picking up (of parts), thereby reducing the operator's cycle time. So by focusing on the red striped bars and the solid red bars, you can potentially perform this work with two operators instead of three.

Reacting to Customer Demand Changes

The other purpose of the wall is to enable an appropriate response when a customer's demands change. Assume, for example, that a customer's original demand was 16 parts/day (480 minutes available per day/16 units = 30 minutes) and that the customer now requires 20 parts/day (480 minutes available per day/20 units = 24 minutes). Given the change, you can lower the takt time line and rebalance.

Frequently, balance walls will be built for various takt times to show the number of operators, their work elements, and how they are balanced when customer demand changes. Figure 9-7 (page 24) is more typical of higher-volume plants; lower-volume plants frequently have shared processes, instead of trying to calculate takt time by conventional methods, do the following:

- Base the time available on the percentage of a machine's availability. For example, if the same assembly cell is occupied 60 percent of the time with other products, it is only available 40 percent of the time, so takt time = (480 minutes × 0.4)/16 units = 12 minutes/unit.

- Take the operator with the highest cycle time and balance the other operators to him or her. Because cycle times should continuously change as improvements are made, you will need to rebalance to the current highest cycle time frequently.

- If you are essentially a job shop and have few forecasted or continuously running products, do not use takt time; instead manage with day-by-hour.

Day-by-Hour Charts

As noted in chapter 4, you can usually expect a 10 percent to 15 percent productivity improvement by utilizing day-by-hour charts, simply by making operators more aware. Creating the charts is the easy part; the more difficult part is changing the behavior of your shopfloor supervisor, who must now review the charts daily and resolve the problems noted on them. If the supervisor fails to monitor the charts for even a single week, operators become frustrated and stop filling in the data.

Day-by-hour charts are especially critical in low-volume plants, where the current production status is hard to understand because of the variety of products built, many of which have different cycle times. Time monitoring also encourages operators to follow an efficient process (that is, standardized work) to ensure parts are completed on time. Remember to introduce day-by-hour to your various processes gradually—start with your biggest bottleneck and move on only when you feel your supervisors can adequately support the day-by-hour charts.

Cross-Trained Team Members

Having team members well trained to perform various jobs helps reduce costs in the following ways:

- Less production loss due to absenteeism, because you have more rebalancing flexibility
- More operators performing a task leads to more involvement in improving it
- More efficient standardized working methods are found by comparing the different ways work elements are performed
- Less ergonomic stress and higher job satisfaction may be achieved through job rotation

When cross-training, put together a current state skills matrix (as discussed in chapter 6) and evaluate where you need further training and standardized work. Then put together a plan to accomplish this. Having this plan allows you to take advantage of slow production periods for training.

Motion Kaizen

Although low-volume plants rarely perform repetitive cycles hundreds of times per day, it is still beneficial to train people in the organization how to improve motions made with the body—or *motion kaizen*. Even though you might manufacture only five to ten pieces each day, you can easily correct a material location or the type of hand tools used, and thus reduce/improve the motions for the remaining production batch and for future orders. Naturally, you need to first observe the job, paying particular attention to the movements of the hands, feet, and eyes.

- When watching the hands, look for long reaches, difficult grips, items that need to be reoriented, poor ergonomic positions, difficult or precise positioning requirements, safety issues, and so on.
- When watching the feet, look for long or unnecessary walks, standing on tiptoe (which is always a safety issue), unnatural positions, slippery surfaces, and so on.
- When watching the eyes, try to see where the operator's attention is focused. If the eyes are spending a lot of time locating parts or tools, reading instructions, or watching out for dangerous moving equipment, they are not focused on building quality into the product.

Ideally, you want your operators to have their materials and tools at the point of use. You are not paying these skilled employees to spend time looking for things; you are paying them to focus attention on the product. Tools and materials should be easy to reach, in a standard location, and correctly orientated. Work standards and specifications should be presented in an easy-to-read format or with pictures that can be quickly understood. All of this allows the operator more time to focus on the product and build in quality.

While you are looking at motion kaizen, you should also be focusing on *material presentation kaizen*, which includes looking at where the material is placed, how easily it is to remove from the packaging, how it is orientated for the operator, and whether any quality issues need to be verified by the operator. Material presentation kaizen goes together with motion kaizen and should be reviewed at the same time.

Teamwork

A *team* is a complete work group that takes a process from a defined starting point to an ending point. Good teams are good because they utilize your resources well. To improve team function and focus, especially while implementing a new system, consider using some of the following strategies:

- Recognize skills and specific knowledge, but have a cross-functional team (utilize the skills matrix in chapter 6 to visualize the cross functionality).

- Educate and communicate the reasons for change. Explain the financial or strategic benefits or why a change in direction is required.

- Allow team members to implement improvements to their own processes.

- Allow the team to organize itself around the work. (The team leader should be responsible for keeping the work standards up to date).

For a team to function efficiently, it should have a team leader. The role and purpose for team leaders was presented in chapter 5, but it is important to accentuate an additional point: Never view a team leader as someone not directly involved in processes. Team leaders are directly involved, because they help your bottom line by eliminating waste from processes and should prove to be one of the most efficient roles in your plant if implemented correctly.

Team boards, which are used by teams to implement and measure improvements, are also a beneficial aspect of teamwork. Aside from encouraging practical adjustments and corrections to processes, team boards encourage initiative and cooperation between teams and management.

Andon Systems

In ancient Japan, *andon* was a paper lantern used as a signaling device over long distances. In twenty-first-century plants, *andon* is an audio and visual communication system that notifies team leaders and supervisors of abnormalities or that support is required. The abnormalities might be quality problems, productivity issues, or machine malfunctions. The purpose of andon is to reduce response time and get the correct support to the problem area, thereby reducing the overall downtime. Andon systems create a sense of urgency, signaling a problem and alerting management that something needs to be done to correct that problem. There are two ways in which andon systems can be activated:

- By a machine automatically detecting an abnormality (this means an operator does not have to watch a machine)
- By an operator noticing something abnormal or needing help and switching on an andon call (a light near the process and a sound to create awareness)

In low-volume plants, the machine-activated andon is typical. The key points to installing the correct hardware that will improve response time and reduce downtime without upsetting the operators are as follows:

- Sound must be used, as operators are not paid to watch lights.
- The sound should be pleasant (music as opposed to buzzers or alarms).
- The sound should function intermittently after the initial warning, as the person responsible may already be occupied on a higher priority issue.
- The team leader should be able to silence the sound quickly and easily.
- Different sounds should be used for different areas of responsibility.
- The andon should be installed in phases, not for an entire plant simultaneously, as not all problems can effectively be supported and resolved.

Note: Because machines stop for a variety of reasons, you may want to have the andon light begin flashing only if a machine is idle for a specified time. This approach will help management recognize if something is a problem; sometimes frequent or short stops of a machine might be a normal condition. An example of an andon light bar with sound added is shown in Figure 9-8, reproduced in color on page 25.

In some sophisticated systems, different signals (different colored lights or different sounds) are used to alert specific people. For example, one kind of signal can be sent if maintenance is needed and another kind of signal can be used to summon production support. If you have team leaders in place, however, start with a simple system that alerts the team leader; he or she can quickly assess whether other support is required.

It is easy to install the hardware for these systems, although benefits will not be realized unless you have trained people available to respond. In other words, do not assume that because the equipment you purchased came with a light that indicates when the machine is stopped, you have an andon system. If no one is assigned to respond to the light or sound signal, the andon system does not exist. It exists only when there is incentive within the organization to make it work as it is intended.

Andon systems are best supported by team leaders, as they are most often available to answer the calls. If they are not filling in for absenteeism, answering andon calls is their first priority. If they are filling in for an absent operator, another available team leader should monitor andon calls from the team.

An andon system can be quite sophisticated; some include a module that can be programmed to send a text message to a manager's mobile phone if a problem has not been resolved after a predetermined period of time (see Figure 9-9). Such escalation procedures need strong management buy-in and are generally used only on bottlenecks.

Figure 9-9. Module to escalate a problem by sending a text message to a manager's/supervisor's cell phone.

All andon systems, no matter how technologically complex or simple, have one basic feature in common: they exist to signal a problem and they reveal,

- the location of bottleneck processes;
- which stations have the most problems;
- where your accumulated downtime is with high technology systems;
- and where abnormalities are occurring.

Summary of Key Points

- Certain improvements affecting manpower must be implemented in a specific order. For example, 5S comes before standardized work, and this can be followed by balance walls. Teamwork with team leaders should precede implementing andon systems.

- Although standardized work can be difficult to apply in low-volume plants, it is critical as the baseline for improvement. Determining the necessary processes to be documented and the format(s) to be used are critical first steps.

- Any time you change a person's work method, you have a temporary negative effect while the operator learns the new method.

- Any process changes require written work standards.

- Operator balance walls encourage the entire team to be involved with improving an area because the waste is easy to see. They also allow easy visualization when the customer changes production requirements (takt time).

- Motion kaizen is a learned skill; by continuously looking for the wastes noted in this section, you will continuously become better at seeing them.

- Teamwork with team leaders is important in implementing many of the lean elements (standardized work, andon, team boards, kanban, and so on). You do not require additional people to fill this role—by eliminating downtime and interruptions, you'll have enough efficiency improvements to pay for the team leader.

- Andon is easy to install but difficult to support. Start implementing slowly, and constantly support the operators in resolving machine problems.

10

Improving Machine Performance and Plant Layout

Certain lean methods apply directly to improving the effectiveness of machines, and the examples presented in this chapter focus on automatic cycling machines. Some of the methods presented can also be applied to processes that do not involve an automatic cycling machine, but most achieve better results when used with machines. A key point to think about is that you can use these methods not just to increase the effectiveness of machinery to increase capacity and sales, but also to avoid unnecessary investment and thereby improve your current ROI (return on investment). The most direct benefits will come from either selling the additional capacity you create or from avoiding unnecessary investment.

Improving your plant layout enhances flow, simplifies management, reduces material handling, and reduces lead time. It can involve simply rearranging an area, installing some U-shaped cells, or undertaking a complete layout change that allows you to switch from functional management to managing by value streams. (Complete layout rearrangements are usually a later step in the lean process because of the cost involved to implement an extensive change; many improvements can be introduced by making some less expensive changes.) This chapter presents a method for layout kaizen.

Overall Equipment Effectiveness

OEE is a useful measurement because it is based on the premise that all losses on machines can be quantified: OEE = availability(%) $\times$ performance(%) $\times$ quality(%). Thus, using OEE helps you determine which process(es) would benefit most from your attention. Many companies separately measure the utilization, output, and quality of a process, but this does not present a total picture of what really counts. Assume, for example, that a stamping machine has the following: availability of 75 percent, output of 80 percent, and quality of 90 percent. Viewed individually, these percentages might not be a reason for concern, but if you look at the combined effect, you see that 75% × 80% × 90% = 54%. This means that you produce a good part only 54 percent of the time, which is and should be a matter of great concern, especially because the individual percentages tend to decrease during the lifecycle of the equipment (older equipment requires more maintenance).

The idea behind OEE, then, is to look cumulatively at all the losses that can occur on a machine or process. It is a standardized measurement that removes allowances—in other words, you do not hide problems by factoring in allowances. In most organizations when there is a major machine breakdown (lasting one or more days), most operators know it and management reacts by trying to minimize the impact and prevent a similar breakdown in the future. However, smaller chronic problems, which account for a majority of the losses on equipment, tend to be accepted as normal. These include tooling problems, feed rates, minor glitches, and so on. These are the issues that OEE highlights and draws attention to.

Issues That Affect OEE

Availability issues might include the following types of downtime:

- Breakdowns (or any unplanned maintenance)
- Changeovers/setups
- Waiting for help (maintenance, team leader, inspection)
- Absenteeism (or other cases of no operators being available)

Performance issues deal with the speeds and feeds of the machine, including the following:

- Running at a slower speed (override is set slower)
- Planned cycle times are not achieved (inferior tooling, machine problems)
- Slow material feed (problems)
- Short stops (to verify tooling, machine parameters)

Quality issues encompass the time lost for material that is out of specification or being reworked, such as the following:

- During startups
- During changeovers
- During regular production

The OEE calculation in more detail:

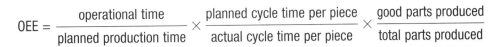

$$OEE = \frac{\text{operational time}}{\text{planned production time}} \times \frac{\text{planned cycle time per piece}}{\text{actual cycle time per piece}} \times \frac{\text{good parts produced}}{\text{total parts produced}}$$

Note: Your lowest OEE is not necessarily the first machine or process to focus on. Instead, you should factor in the locations of your bottlenecks and consider other business priorities, like upcoming changes in customer forecasts. Most importantly, as mentioned in chapter 5, you should never allow someone in your organization to dissuade you from using OEE by presenting "uptime" numbers that likely include allowances for certain problems.

How to Use OEE

There are a number of reasons to monitor and improve overall equipment effectiveness. OEE, for example, helps you create additional capacity, avoid purchasing new equipment, and reduce costs. The following is a step-by-step discussion of how to reduce costs on existing processes.

1. Define how OEE will be calculated and begin monitoring it on the processes you consider critical (or on your bottlenecks). Daily tracking is recommended. Use a visual display format and set a goal, when possible (see Figure 10-1, reproduced in color on page 26). Also display (on a chart) how you are calculating OEE. Because old machines, especially those with poor TPM, have lower OEE, it is helpful to include the year the machine was manufactured on the chart.

2. Include some data analysis of the causes for low OEE; this is usually best displayed with a Pareto chart. You can separate the reasons for lost time by availability, performance, and quality or group them together as shown in Figure 10-2.

3. You can now form problem-solving teams and assign responsibilities. Remember to prioritize and tackle bottlenecks, areas requiring investment, or other priorities in your plant.

There are many solutions and tools to improve OEE (for example, SMED, 5S, standardized work). Because maintenance issues are frequently at the top of the list, one solution is better TPM, which is discussed in the following section.

Total Productive Maintenance

TPM is the overall process of stabilizing equipment, thereby increasing availability, performance, and quality. A multifaceted process that adapts to various circumstances, total productive maintenance often functions as preventive main-

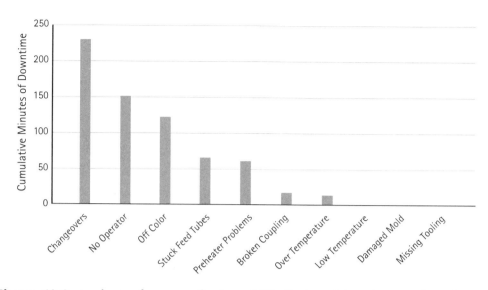

Figure 10-2. Analysis of reasons for low OEE displayed in a Pareto chart format.

tenance and predictive maintenance. Because the goal is to improve equipment reliability and maintain an acceptable level of reliability, you must constantly learn about the equipment. This requires frequent information updates because there will be constant changes as the equipment continues to age. The process will involve support from operators and the maintenance department.

Note: Not all low-volume plants have separate maintenance staffs. Instead, some use subcontractors to perform periodic maintenance and repairs. These subcontractors often have considerable experience with your type of machines, and this experience should be incorporated into your TPM plan (even if this involves paying for technicians' time to help develop your plan).

Traditional maintenance systems do not have good data-gathering or root-cause analysis in place. They may be proud of their ability to fight fires ("saving the day"); there is little operator involvement, so operators feel no ownership; and spare parts and tooling are not well organized. TPM's strength is that it precludes fighting fires, makes operators part of an ongoing monitoring and maintenance system, and is designed to work in an organized environment.

OEE helps you prioritize TPM opportunities and categorize particular pieces of equipment. A low availability percentage (in your OEE measurement) usually indicates TPM opportunities, although performance and quality are also affected by poor maintenance of the equipment. TPM will help stabilize an area by doing the following:

- Reducing unscheduled downtime
- Simplifying and shortening the time for performing maintenance tasks
- Involving the operator in maintaining the equipment
- Quickly clarifying normal and abnormal conditions

- Teaching operators to be proactive

To implement TPM, do the following:

- Either from your team boards or your OEE measurement, identify the problems that are equipment related.
- Prioritize the problems (use Pareto charts).
- Correlate these problems with any existing planned maintenance procedures and any periodic maintenance recommended by the equipment manufacturer.
- Make an initial list of maintenance to be performed and the frequency.
- Schedule an organized event with the operators, team leaders, maintenance department, and supervisors to clean and restore the equipment. During this event, the following should be put in place:
  - Visually show normal versus abnormal conditions in critical areas. Some examples of how this can be accomplished are shown in Figure 10-3.

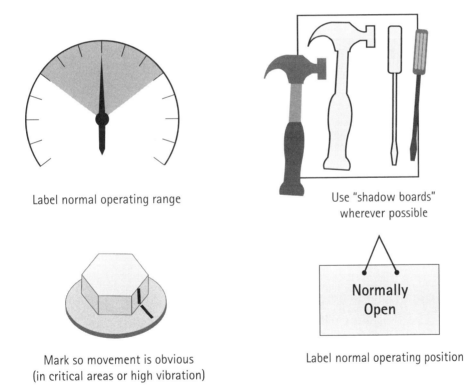

Label normal operating range

Use "shadow boards" wherever possible

Mark so movement is obvious (in critical areas or high vibration)

Normally Open

Label normal operating position

Figure 10-3. Visualizing normal (versus abnormal) on the machine is part of TPM.

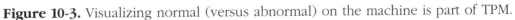

  - Add additional maintenance items to existing list (some of these will surface while the team is cleaning, restoring, and visually marking the machine) and the recommended frequency (consult an external technician, if applicable).

- Take the newly developed master list of recommended maintenance items and decide which can be performed by the production operator and which should be performed by maintenance or outsourced maintenance. Clarify frequencies for all items to be performed (see Figure 10-4).

Task	Frequency	Production or maintenance	Standard procedure written	Required time to complete
Fill lubrication oil	Daily	Production	Yes	5 min.
Fill cutting fluid	Daily	Production	Yes	10 min.
Check/clean air filters	Daily	Production	No	
Replace bearings on X axis	100 hrs	Maintenance	Yes	3.2 hours
Replace bearings on Y axis	100 hrs	Maintenance	Yes	3 hours
Check/replace motor brushes on X, Y & Z drives	75 hrs	Maintenance	No	
Lubricate bearings on main spindle	100 hrs	Maintenance	No	

Figure 10-4. Master list of maintenance items for a machine.

- Write standardized work for tasks if they have not previously been written (refer to chapter 9). It is recommended that you include the time required in your standardized work format, especially for the planned tasks performed by maintenance (these tend to be performed without work standards or without a timeframe; therefore, there is usually a lot of opportunity for improvement). Make certain that the work standards are supplemented with pictures (see Figure 10-5).

- Ensure necessary parts and supplies are on hand and are properly set up as stock items.

- Ensure all tooling is readily available (not hidden in cabinets but openly displayed).

- Ensure production operators and maintenance are trained to do the standardized work.

- Put in place an audit system. This may include operators signing off on the board, maintenance calendars with sign-offs, and/or production and maintenance supervisor audits (see chapter 2).

Understand that this is not the end. Every time there is a problem with a machine, you need to ask whether there is some way to avoid having the

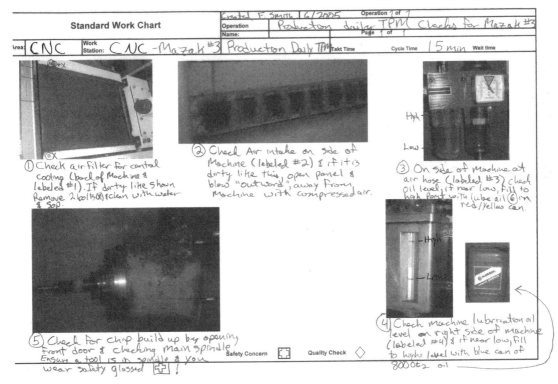

Figure 10-5. Standardized worksheet for a preventative maintenance procedure.

problem recur. Can you be proactive, add a new item to your TPM procedure, and avoid future occurrences?

Machine Kaizen

Machine kaizen is designed to shorten a machine's cycle time. Take this approach only after you have improved the process and the flow, as machine kaizen frequently requires investment. You should always begin with improving the non-value-added operations, since most opportunities lie there, and then move to the value-added (machine time) operations. Many companies become interested in improving machines before they have worked on flow and process improvements, because machine improvements frequently involve technical solutions—and let's face it: Technical solutions are easier and more interesting to implement than process changes, which usually require a change in human behavior. Take, for example, a machine that has a lot of opportunity in setup; rather than focusing on this, an engineer is more likely to become interested in reducing the door-opening time by four seconds per cycle by installing higher-speed pneumatics. In the end, he is able to show less than a one-year payback on the investment. Setup can be easily reduced by fifteen minutes per cycle, which is clearly a better productivity improvement—and requires no investment. So although the engineering improvement is important, it should be a lower priority and its importance should be based on the "performance" percentage (in the OEE calculation) and Pareto chart analysis.

Ironically, shortening a machine's cycle time by chaning the working method is sometimes more difficult to accomplish than complex engineering changes because it involves changing a method. That means you must change or modify some of the tools you have been using and also change the way your people work. Some items to look for when improving machine cycle times follow:

- The feed and speed rates in the programs may be too slow. If your programmer has worked for many years in your organization, is the only programmer, or was trained in-house, you might want to randomly check a program for a high-volume part with an external expert to see whether significant differences are found (periodically re-tooling, using different program methods, programming shorter and faster robot moves, and so on). Often, when problems arise, a temporary solution involves slowing down the machine; the machine may continue operating at this slower speed without anyone seeking or resolving the root cause.

- A machine is used to quality check or deburr parts while operators are standing and waiting. Always be clear about which processes can be done manually, what your capacity requirements are, and how much time the operator is waiting.

- Poor fixture design can lead to longer loading times, slowing machine speeds because of vibration or scrap, and slower changeover time. Poor fixture placement can also lead to slower changeover times.

- On higher-volume processes, indexing or loading movements should also be reviewed; for example, the speed to unload a part, how far a door should open, and so on. See the example in Figure 10-6.

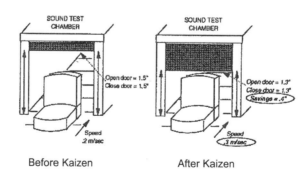

Figure 10-6. Reducing a machine's cycle time by looking at its loading movements.

- You have a way to detect abnormalities, especially before the machine stops. Warning systems that were not originally incorporated into the machine might be added if they are justified; for example, low fluid or material warnings, high temperature warnings, and so on.

Changeover Time and SMED

Your machine productivity is improved with shorter changeover times. In OEE, the changeover time is not considered as productive time. Instead, the time is subtracted from your "availability." Although changeover is necessary (and usually performed more frequently in low-volume plants), it is not allotted for in the "availability" portion when the OEE is calculated; therefore, it is not included in the time for producing good parts. By not including setup time as part of a machine's productive time, you highlight the need to reduce changeover, most likely using SMED (see chapter 8).

Shift Patterns

Shift patterns can be difficult to balance. Because the cycle times of the various processes utilized in making a product are rarely well balanced, you frequently have unbalanced workloads. For example, to produce one part requires three hours of lathe time, one hour of milling time, and twenty minutes of assembly time. If demand is such that you need the lathe to operate on two or three shifts per day, you might require the mill and assembly for less than one shift per day, making scheduling and one-piece flow difficult. Because of the capital costs for equipment, machines often run on more than one shift, whereas manual processes, such as assembly, are usually performed during a single shift.

Further complicating shift patterns are production requirements that do not fit into eight-hour time blocks. For example, when capacity requirements are for eleven hours a day instead of eight hours a day, you add a second shift to use the machine three more hours—then you have to utilize the extra five hours of the second-shift operator elsewhere.

In low-volume plants, the difficulty is compounded by a frequently changing schedule (see Figure 10-7), so the day-to-day balancing between processes needs to be accomplished through your organization's flexibility (cross-training, overtime, kaizen). When a particular process is frequently overloaded, review all options presented in this book before adding a partially utilized shift. To improve your shift patterns, work on the following:

- Analyze all reasons for low OEE and start an action plan.
- Reduce changeover time.
- Reduce load and unload time.
- Reduce machine cycle time (machine kaizen).
- Reduce quality problems.

- Reduce absenteeism.
- Manage the overloaded process as a bottleneck.

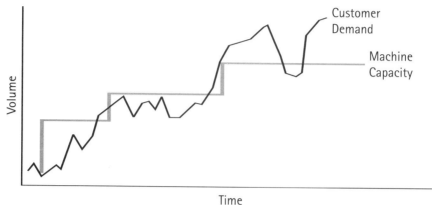

Figure 10-7. Problems caused in low-volume plants by adding shifts to offset frequently changing demand.

Layout Kaizen

Layout kaizen is used to improve the production flow. It can be utilized to achieve the following:

- Reduce lead time.
- Simplify management of the area (allow better visual management and value stream management).
- Improve flow (eliminate the need for large batch production).
- Reduce material movement and inventory.
- Identify bottlenecks.
- Utilize shared processes more efficiently.

Some high-mix plants find that as the demand for some part numbers increases, it is better to separate those parts and assemble them in discrete areas that are more efficiently set up. You may choose to rearrange an area or create a flow redesign for the entire plant, the latter of which is often done if a plant is changing from managing by process (where processes are grouped together—stamping, welding, assembly) to managing by value stream (where you group together all processes related to a product—machined valves versus control cabinets). Other layout ideas may include U-shaped cells for more flexibility or grouping together similar processes. Whichever you choose, it is important to explain your reasons for changing the layout to those who will be affected by the change.

Layout kaizen is usually recommended after you have completed flow, process, and machine improvements, because the process is involved and can be expensive. Many have learned the hard way that making major layout changes before implementing other lean elements can be disastrous, mostly because as you start to connect unreliable process (those with low OEE) and remove the WIP that hid their inefficiencies, you actually reduce your capacity. So fix low OEEs first, and then change your layout.

Keep in mind that your current layout has probably evolved to accommodate products and processes that have been added as your business has grown and changed; it is not likely to reflect some master plan based on the flow of all your current products and capacities. Below, we examine some common ways to improve layout: correlation matrices, current and future layouts with flow lines, and balance walls (which are also discussed in chapter 9). The basic steps for improving an existing layout are shown in Figure 10-8.

Step 5 in Figure 10-8 (setting up a correlation matrix and rating relationship system) is important, so an example is shown in Figure 10-9.

Any shared machines or processes that have an important relationship with other processes should also be noted in the correlation matrix. These shared processes should be located as centrally as possible to all the processes they supply. In your layout drawings, use a separate color to indicate shared processes.

Current State Layout

In Figure 10-10, you see long, thick dark lines; these are opportunities for improvement. Long lines indicate long distance movements. Thick lines signal problems with movement: they indicate either that too many trips are being taken to move material or that large/heavy material is being moved. Both are to be avoided.

In Figure 10-10 (page 164), you also see lots of lines crossing each other and a lot of space   used for storage; these are additional opportunities for improvement.

Future State Layout

Taking into account your objectives for Step 6 in Figure 10-8 (develop five layout alternatives), draw five rough layouts. Five layouts are recommended because the first three alternatives most people create are easy and comfortable; you need to stretch yourself and allow yourself to move away from this easy and comfortable position. Once you have all five layout alternatives, select the one that best meets your objectives and draw in the thick and thin flow

---

STEPS FOR LAYOUT KAIZEN

1. Define Project

___ Objectives (specific targets)

___ Scope (size of area to be included)

___ Team members identified

___ Target dates for 8 steps defined

___ Determine how to track progress and store information

2. Scope of project

___ Determine budget

___ Identify any monuments (equipment that is considered unmovable)

___ Any new technologies to be introduced

___ New "lean" elements to be introduced

3. Gather data

___ Current & future capacities by product type (include dates)

___ List any new products planned for introduction

___ Current and future machine capacities

___ Any special equipment requirements (ventilation, pits, electrical power, etc.)

___ Other process capacities (i.e., assembly line)

___ Layout to scale of available area (AutoCAD)

___ Current & future equipment to scale

___ Process flows, previous & following process steps

___ Note all shared processes and which processes they supply with material

4. Current state value stream maps

___ Create or review current state value stream maps

___ Look for current problems with material flow

___ Look for current problems with information flow

___ Consider if value stream management (instead of functional management) is feasible

___ Note build-to-order parts (MRP) "strangers"

___ Note kanban parts "runners" (should they be in a cell?)

___ Note current levels & desired levels of inventory

___ Sketch future state value stream map

5. Rank the correlation between physical locations of processes

___ Set up correlation matrix

___ Complete rating relationships between 1–5 points

6. Develop 5 or more rough layout alternatives

___ Use general process groupings

___ Draw in flow arrows (thick lines for high volume or heavy material, thin lines for low volume)

___ Ensure all considerations from steps 1-5 have been taken into account

___ Additional considerations: clean vs. dirty areas, alternative or additional shipping & receiving points, nerve center for visual management, general visual management considerations, machine accessibility, material handling areas, tugger routes, pull systems, separate material handling personnel, "U" cells, outsourcing vs. in house

___ Draw a "work balance wall" for any cells that need to have the workloads balanced

___ Complete an advantage/disadvantage analysis of each alternative

___ Show shared processes in a separate color & show flow areas to all processes they feed

7. Select 2 alternatives for detailed layouts

___ Complete detailed to-scale layouts

___ Identify locations of all considerations agreed upon in steps 1–6

___ Draw in flow arrows (thick lines for high volume or heavy material, thin lines for low volume)

___ Determine how "lean" elements will be introduced in this layout

___ Compare both alternatives to objectives

8. Select final layout

___ List advantages/disadvantages

___ Note all lean elements considered in new layout

___ Note how visual management will be enhanced

___ Prepare implementation steps with timing

___ Estimate costs

___ Submit to management for final approval

Figure 10-8. Steps for layout kaizen.

CORRELATION MATRIX

Correlation Scale

1 = No relationship   2 = Not important   3 = Important   4 = Very important   5 = Critical

	General Receiving	Die storage	Press/Stamping	Raw materials stamping	Raw materials machining	Machining	Toolroom (Die repair)	Work-in-process (WIP)	Machine product assembly	Stamped product assembly	Shipping
General Receiving											
Die storage	5										
Press/Stamping	2	5									
Raw materials stamping	5	2	5								
Raw materials machining	3	1	1	2							
Machining	2	1	1	1	5						
Toolroom (die repair)	3	5	3	3	1	1					
Work-in-process (WIP)	1	1	3	2	1	2	1				
Machine product assembly	4	1	1	1	2	4	1	4			
Stamped product assembly	4	2	4	2	1	1	2	4	3		
Shipping	1	2	1	1	1	1	2	1	4	4	

The ▨ in the correlation matrix are the important relationships that the proposed "future state layout" takes into account.

Figure 10-9. Example of a correlation matrix.

lines (See Figure 10-11). Although all lean methods should be considered in the future state layout, the most important is flow. Work toward the ideal state of one-piece flow, pulling in as many lean concepts as you can.

In the future state map presented in the figure, you can see the following improvements:

- By adding two shipping doors, you can directly ship from assembly, thus eliminating finished goods storage and reducing the shipping area.

- Dividing assembly into two separate value streams allows one value stream manager to be responsible for the machining area all the way to the machined valve assembly area and another manager to be responsible for stamping all the way to the control cabinet assembly area. In this way, you are managing by product instead of process.

- Replacing the work-in-process area by putting in a pull system (kanban) from the assembly supermarket to machining and stamping saves floor space, inventory, and the labor necessary to schedule those parts.

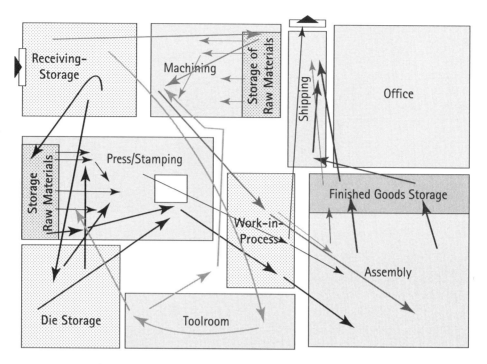

Figure 10-10. Current state layout with flow lines.

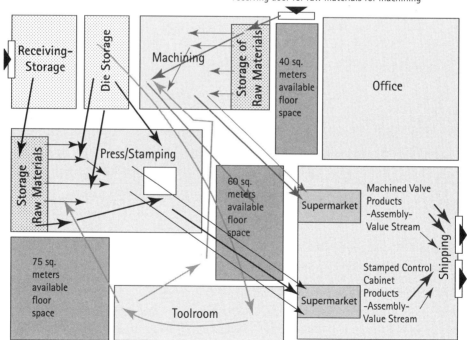

Figure 10-11. Future state layout with flow lines.

- Reducing the space required in the receiving and storage area by using kanban with the suppliers and relocating die storage reduces the distance to move large dies.

- In total, 175 square meters of floor space can be made available.
- You see that some of the long thick flow lines have been eliminated, meaning less time is spent moving materials.

If you are doing layout kaizen to regroup work or put separate processes together in a U-shaped cell, you will need to look at the balance between the work. This will allow you to see how much rebalancing is necessary and how you will benefit from changing the layout. (See Figure 10-12; see also explanation of how to make a balance wall in chapter 9.)

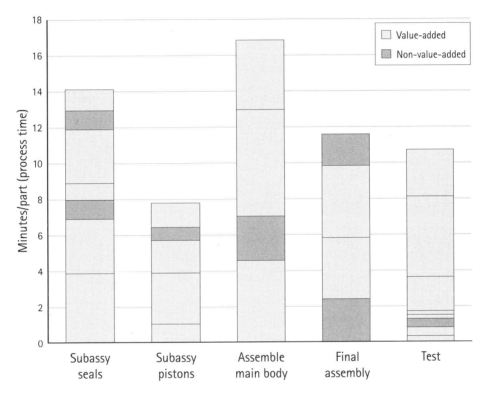

Figure 10-12. Making a balance wall before reorganizing into a U-shaped cell.

In Figure 10-12, assume that the differences in process times are currently hidden by WIP inventory. If you are going to group these five operations into a cell, you need to rebalance these processes. In low-volume plants, you would most likely set the cell up based on a family of parts. Also consider the following:

- The ideas from the future state need to be analyzed with some type of a cost-benefit analysis.
- An action plan should be developed using a plan-do-check-act method (like the action plan shown near the end of chapter 12).
- All objectives should be verified after the future state is realized and work standards should be written for all affected processes.

Summary of Key Points

- OEE is a superior measurement because it looks cumulatively at all factors affecting a process, and it is a standardized approach.

- OEE indicates where to concentrate your efforts.

- Where to focus your TPM effort should come from OEE tracking. Remember to write standardized work (including the element times) for all production and maintenance procedures.

- Machine kaizen usually involves capital expenditures, so it should be considered only after flow and process improvements (which rarely require capital expenditures).

- Layout kaizen often involves capital expenditures, so it should be considered after flow improvements, process improvements, and machine improvements are made, unless you have a specific business need (for example, you are changing to value stream management, you need additional floor space, or you have a particularly poor layout causing extra material handling).

- Before increasing the number of shifts on which a machine is utilized, try improving the process to create additional capacity, using the methods discussed in this chapter.

11

Making Improvements through Office Department Kaizen

When companies implement lean, they usually start by looking at the shop floor, hoping to find savings by reducing direct labor. The next area targeted is indirect labor on the shop floor, even though this is more difficult to quantify in terms of tasks and savings. One area that most companies going lean have a hard time visualizing as a target for improvement is the office. Although this area, under normal conditions, seems to be busy, it is hard to quantify the tasks office personnel are performing and the value they are adding.

Dealing with departments means dealing with people, and one aspect of this is the number of people. If, for example, you had sales of $10 million last year with a staff of 20 and your sales today (with the same 20 people) are at $8 million. Proportionately, and assuming that everything else remains the same (for example, order size), it seems to make sense that you now need a staff of only 16, and most companies would see reducing the number of people as quite logical. On the other hand, when sales increase, most companies do not rush out and hire additional staff; they try to cope with the existing staff until someone complains loudly enough or critical work begins to fall through the cracks.

There is a better way to understand the office workload and make improvements, and this chapter shows how. The main thrust is to introduce a method that will improve a particular *department* in the office: one that management feels offers opportunities for improvement, is a current bottleneck, has a long lead time, or appears inefficient. (If management's target is a particular office process rather than a department, see chapter 12.) The method, office department kaizen, has numerous benefits:

- It reduces lead time within the department
- It allows more time to focus on the critical issues with less time spent on non-value-added activities
- It allows you to increase the responsibility or scope of the department
- It looks to reduce the size and cost of the department
- It allows you to process more work through the department

As with any methodology, office department kaizen works best when those implementing have a clear understanding about the current state. Thus, before you begin, you need to understand the following about the targeted office department:

- Time spent completing a task (processing time)
- Time spent waiting (waiting time)
- Percent of time information is complete and accurate for incoming work
- Percent of time information is complete and accurate for outgoing work (represents the quality of the department's work)

The Kaizen Method

The steps for conducting office department kaizen are rather simple but might cause apprehension within the department if their purpose is not clearly explained. First, you must choose a department (e.g., purchasing, planning, or engineering) where you think opportunities exist. It's important for management to clarify the reason this department was chosen; that is, you must identify a specific opportunity for improvement. It is equally important to set a specific goal (for example, improve customer service by 1 percent per month, reduce delays to less than 4 per week, reduce cost 2 percent per month for a total of 10 percent, and so on).

Because you probably do not have any real data on how people in the department spend their time, you can begin by asking department personnel to keep diaries and note activities over a period of time in small time increments. Then, schedule a meeting with a facilitator for those that have maintained the diaries. The facilitator is usually someone who is not connected with the department, but who has experience in leading this type of activity, and the times from the diaries are categorized and incorporated into Pareto charts (see Figure 11-1). The data can then be discussed and analyzed by the group and decisions can be made on how to reach the goal set by management.

The example in the Pareto chart in Figure 11-1 shows how time was spent by people working in a small purchasing department. The figure illustrates what is typically found in most departments: Most people (most of the time)

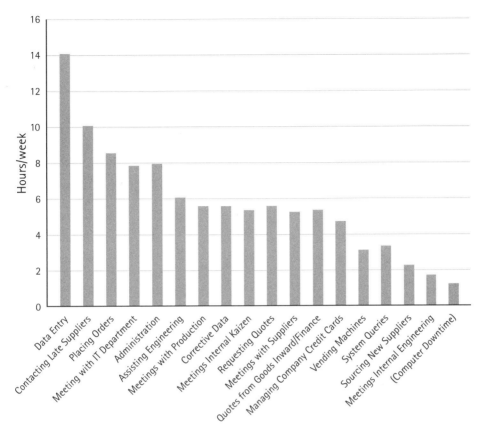

Figure 11-1. How the purchasing department spends its time.

are engaged in non-value-added or administrative tasks instead of on core tasks or improvements. The figure shows that the team spends most of its time on "data entry" and "contacting late suppliers"; ideally, the primary focus should be "sourcing new suppliers" and "requesting quotes." Other issues in a typical office department include the following:

- End-of-the-month panic
- In-bound trays that do not utilize first-in, first-out, so some paperwork is delayed
- Lack of training (or lack of a training method), so personnel are instructed only to watch how someone else performs the process
- Batching paperwork
- People creating their own systems because they do not trust the official system

The Steps for an Office Kaizen

The best way to conduct an office department kaizen is to follow a series of interrelated and sequential steps. The step-by-step instructions are listed below:

1. Hold an introductory meeting to explain the purpose, why the department has been chosen, and the expected outcome. The following should be discussed at this meeting:

   a. Introduce the diary. Show examples and explain that detailed notations must be made daily for a minimum of two weeks (three to four weeks is better).

   b. Explain that these diaries should be kept in small time increments (usually no more than 15 minutes) during the normal workday (see Figure 11-2). This structure makes it easy for staff to enter data frequently throughout the day. Make it clear that no diary should be completed from memory at the end of the day.

Name: *Larry Jones*   Date: *Jan 17*

Time	Activity	Comments/Improvements
7:00–7:15	*Check e-mail*	
7:15–7:30	*Check e-mail*	*Better spam filter*
7:30–7:45	*Revise dwg 6554*	
7:45–8:00	*Revise dwg 6554*	
8:00–8:15	*Revise dwg 6554*	
8:15–8:30	*Phone call asking how to find a file.*	
8:30–8:45	*Read specification 33456*	
8:45–9:00	*Read specification 34456*	

Figure 11-2. Example of a diary.

   c. A few days after the diaries are begun, hold a brief question and answer session.

   d. After gathering data, hold a departmental workshop to analyze the data and determine actions to be taken. Make sure to restate the goals (an example might be, "reduce the time spent on activities determined to be non-value-added so you can source up to three new suppliers each week").

   e. Show how you plan to measure success (see Figure 11-3).

2. After two days of diary writing, review to see what problems office personnel are encountering and clear up the following:

   a. What should be included

   b. How detailed it should be

   c. A few examples of basic activity categories

Note: Do not create specific categories on what you assume takes place in the department. Taking this approach will result in fewer notes on actual

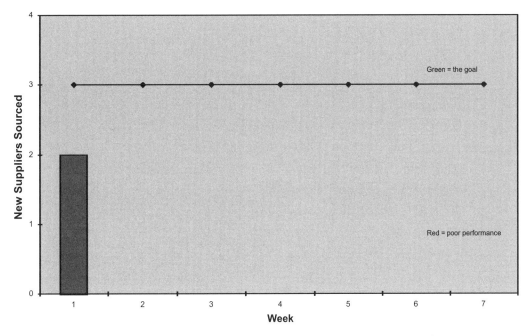

Figure 11-3. Example of how success will be measured.

activities because people find it easier to list tasks in categories rather than describe what they actually did. Experience shows that better results are achieved if everyone keeps notes on how time is actually spent; the data can be categorized during the workshop.

3. Start the workshop, making sure to do the following:

  a. Reemphasize the goal.

  b. Group data into activity/function/process categories, using between fifteen and twenty specific categories

  c. Show categories in Pareto format.

  d. Decide whether the activity categories where the most time is spent are indeed the most important for the department.

  e. Decide whether too much time is spent on a particular activity (for example, meetings, data entry, and so on).

  f. List problems within these activity categories (for example, data entry is slow because unnecessary data is required, or there are requirements for separate paper archives when everything is kept in a secure database).

  g. Perform a flow analysis: Chart or map difficult and problematic processes. Decide which processes require more in-depth understanding and improvements. Plan to conduct an office process kaizen (see chapter 12).

h. Write improvement ideas and place these ideas into the correct area on an impact versus difficulty matrix (see Figure 11-4). Taking this step prioritizes ideas and turns them into an action list. Those ideas that are easy to implement and have high impact should be addressed first.

i. Write an action list of what needs to be done to reduce time spent on non-value-added activities or to reduce unnecessary processes, prioritizing on the basis of what the impact versus difficulty matrix reveals. Quantify the expected time savings for each applicable action.

j. Determine activity/function/process categories that you want office personnel to spend more time on.

k. Discuss how the time saved can now be utilized more productively.

Impact – Difficulty Matrix

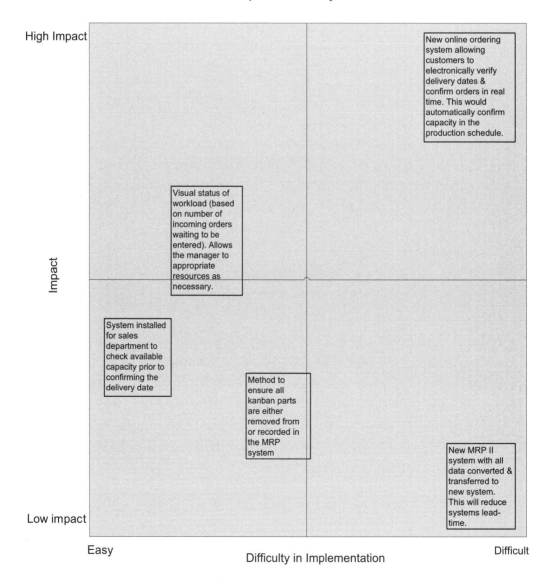

Figure 11-4. Impact versus difficulty matrix.

Further Suggestions

- Prior to the workshop, have a manager benchmark or visit other plants that have similar processes or activities.

- At the end of the workshop, do the following.
  - Create a loose structure for moving forward.
  - Decide on individuals' responsibilities. Document procedures with standardized work.
  - Determine how success will be measured (the metrics).

- After the workshop, immediately start working on the action list and review each week.

Examples of Understanding the Detail within a Particular Process or Task

Once you have determined processes or tasks that require further understanding, evaluation, or investigation, you can use the methods shown in the examples discussed below:

Complicated Problems within a Department

When tasks that stay within the department involve quite a few steps, draw the steps out in a flowchart format. Then, question the necessity for each step and/or determine whether improvements can be made to the individual step. Use colored markers to highlight opportunities and problems. You should also consider including the average process time (PT) for completing the task, the average wait time (WT), and the percentage of time information arrives completely and accurately (C&A).

- The *process time* is the actual working time required to complete one unit; for example, the data entry time for one purchase order is four minutes, so this is the processing time.

  Note: The Maynard Operation Sequence Technique (known as MOST) was mentioned in chapter 9 as a simple method that utilizes a predetermined motion time system to determine standard times. It also contains a quick and simple method to determine times for administrative tasks called AdminMOST. More information can be obtained from the Internet. Your other option is observation, or asking those responsible to monitor and record the times.

- The *wait time* begins when a task is released from one process and then sits waiting for the next process to begin. Wait time includes the time to batch process. If, for example, a computer process like MRP is involved, and it runs the batch every night, include the nightly run: The wait time, then, would likely be one day.

- The percentage of *complete and accurate* involves looking at how often the work passed to the next process is not missing any information or does not contain mistakes. Examples of incomplete work are calls that must be made to clarify something, missing necessary information, missing signatures or dates, and so on. Inaccuracy issues might include incorrect data, prices, dates, suppliers, technical specifications, and others.

Figure 11-5 is the detailed mapping of one task for a production control department. All processes that the team was concerned about are shaded gray, and kaizen suggestions are shown with the blitzes ![KAIZEN]. It is recommended that the process times, wait times, and percent of time the information is complete and accurate are included. Although gathering this data requires some effort, it almost always highlights opportunities. You may be surprised by how often requests (or tasks) are sent without complete and accurate data, and by the amount of time people spend chasing and correcting information. When you map the process, you can see ideas for improvements almost immediately. Two good ideas for a process map follow:

- Highlight value-add steps, so that it becomes clear how many steps do not add value. You can begin by focusing on the non-value-adding activities.
- Include a photocopy of the forms or data-entry screens utilized at the various steps to identify improvement opportunities.

You can quickly map out a flowchart using sticky-back notes. Colors can be used to represent different categories of activity: In Figure 11-6, reproduced in color on page 26, yellow shows process steps, orange shows where decisions are required, and red shows problems or improvement ideas.

Processes that Cross into Other Departments

A process may involve more than one department; for example, an engineering change may affect placing a purchase order or changing a production schedule. Often, the process flow within a department experiences few delays, but when it is handed off to the next department, delays do occur. A lot of control is lost when responsibility moves from one department to another and a process must wait for operators or equipment to become available. This situation usually presents great opportunities for improvement through a method called office process kaizen. A graphic representation of *office process kaizen* is presented in Figure 11-7.

With six different departments involved, it is not hard to imagine how an ordinary procedure can slow down and take many days to complete. Note that the illustration includes process time and wait time as well as complete and accurate percentages (C&A%). Sometimes, visualizing the process in this format allows a team to see problems and potential improvements clearly. (A more detailed discussion on office process kaizen is presented in chapter 12.)

Scheduling an order

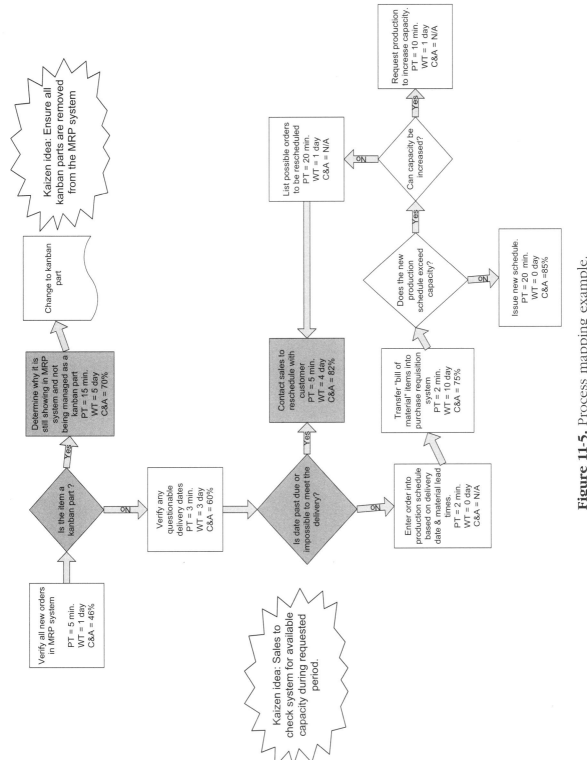

Figure 11-5. Process mapping example.

175

Set up & order new part

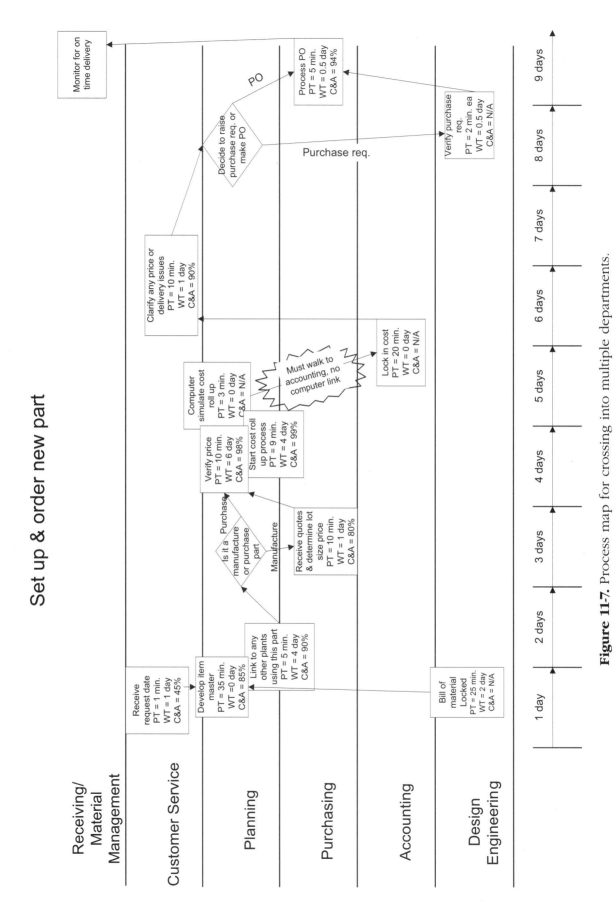

Figure 11-7. Process map for crossing into multiple departments.

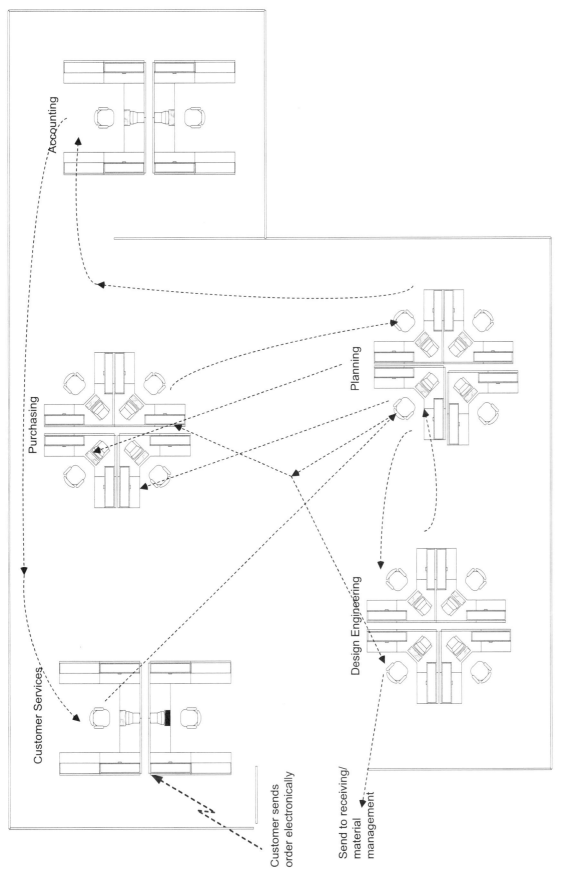

Figure 11-8. Spaghetti diagram.

Accounting

Purchasing

Planning

Customer Services

Design Engineering

Customer sends
order electronically

Send to receiving/
material
management

Note: Factors within your control should be your highest priority. A final step for office process kaizen is to draw a spaghetti diagram (see Figure 11-8) that shows the physical flow of a document (or process) and to identify improvements. If the dashed lines following the flow resemble a plate of spaghetti, look for opportunities.

Summary of Key Points

- To improve a department, you need to understand how people spend their time; this is best achieved by having each office employee complete a diary.

- Diaries can be used to analyze which tasks need a more detailed analysis and which tasks need to be improved.

- Those tasks/processes identified for improvement can then be mapped; mapping identifies problems and generates ideas for improvement.

- Once certain processes are improved, they require less time, which gives the department more time for new tasks or increased focus on existing tasks. The goals should be clearly stated, and the method for tracking goal attainment should be clearly defined.

- A better understanding of how different departments spend their time also helps you understand your actual costs and can make cost allocation more precise.

- In many cases, you will find significant time lost during a process because the previous process was not performed completely and accurately.

- Remember to write standardized work (see chapter 9) for any processes you change or any new processes you put in place.

12

Making Improvements through Office Process Kaizen

If you are aware of a particular process (versus an entire department) in the office that is always late, produces poor quality work, has a long lead time, or generally need's improvement, implement an office process kaizen. This is also a good method to implement if you have already begun an office department kaizen and have discovered that a particular process crosses departmental boundaries.

In many low-volume and job-shop businesses, significant time is spent processing paperwork—sometimes as much as 50 percent of the employees work in the office. The percentage of people and time are greater than it would be in a high-volume business with regularly repeating orders, so even small improvements can have a big impact. There are four general benefits of improving an office process:

- Reduces lead time, which generally helps increase sales
- Allows the work order more time in the production schedule
- Reduces cost
- Creates available time

Before you begin to implement office process kaizen, take a long hard look at your employees and the activities they are engaged in. Never assume that the current size of your staff or its high level of activity is necessary or acceptable. Although everyone may seem busy—even overloaded—this may be a result of lots of non-value-added activity.

As you work to improve various office processes, you want to standardize and quantify the time necessary to complete them. This will lead to improvements and make it possible to quantify a time (and, therefore, a cost) for these processes. (Knowing the time and cost allows you to understand your overhead costs better, which, in turn, means that you may be able to factor in a more precise cost when determining your sales price.)

Where to Start: Inputting an Order

If no other opportunities have been identified, a good process to start with is order input, a typical process that involves various departments in most companies. Generally, the opportunities discovered here are reflective of opportunities elsewhere. When mapping order input, do not include the quoting process because quoting is a separate process that consumes significant time, is subject to factors beyond your control, and should be mapped separately. For any office process, including, order input, you want to understand the following:

- Time spent completing a task (processing time)
- Time spent waiting (waiting time)
- Percent of time information is complete and accurate for incoming work
- Percent of time information is complete and accurate for outgoing work (represents the quality of the preceding process's work)

Figure 12-1 shows a typical example of the major steps for entering a new order into the system. In this example, it takes about nine days on the average before an order is placed in the schedule and production can start; there is no significant waiting time between processes (for example, waiting for engineering to sign off or for a purchasing manager's approval), although some companies do experience significant wait time. Remember that waiting and having to complete or explain incomplete and inaccurate information are the primary inefficiencies, especially when a process moves between departments.

In the process steps shown in Figure 12-1, most factors are within your control, and you can see how the processing time is spent within the departments and how much waiting time exists when handing over responsibilities to another department. You can also see whether and how often the preceding processes are providing complete and accurate information. Focus on the three steps:

1. Reduce the amount of incomplete and inaccurate information.
2. Reduce waiting time (usually between departments or processes).
3. Reduce process time.

If the teams cannot agree on how long it takes to complete a set of given tasks, have team members record time from two to three cycles of the task and then complete the mapping afterward. If you hear anyone on the team saying,

Processing an Order

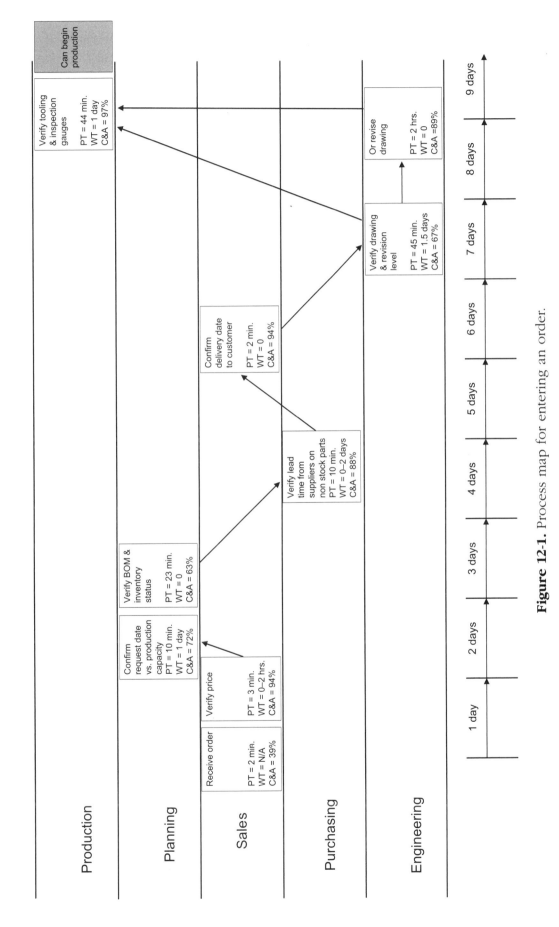

Figure 12-1. Process map for entering an order.

"I do it this way," you have an immediate opportunity to standardize the work with the agreed-upon best method. Keep in mind, however, that the best method is only the current best method, and you should always be looking for ways to improve it.

Reducing Incomplete and Inaccurate Information

You may be surprised by how often a task is passed on with missing information or mistakes. If you look at the first task in Figure 12-1, which is "receive order," you see that the information is complete and accurate only 39 percent of the time. This may reflect poorly presented information in your catalog, a poorly trained sales force, or a poorly designed order form. In any case, some problem solving is needed.

Try to quantify how much time is spent collecting and correcting this incomplete and inaccurate information. Doing so can help prioritize which process to start with if you have various processes with a low percentage of complete and accurate.

In many cases, various functions within an organization may disagree about how complete and accurate the information is, but without data, such disagreements are moot; generally nothing changes and living with the situation becomes accepted as part of the job.

Reducing Wait Time

To reduce wait time, take the following steps:

1. Set a goal for a shorter wait time. Develop a daily tracking chart.

2. Determine how many similar requests in the queue can wait before wait time exceeds the new goal. (It might be necessary to separate requests into different categories depending on the time or difficulty involved). Ensure all queues work with first-in, first-out.

3. Set up a visual system that immediately displays when the quantity of requests waiting to be processed will exceed the capacity of the department to process them within the newly determined wait time. In some cases, parameters can be programmed into the computer (if your system allows), but a simple visual system can work well.

In Figure 12-1, the purchasing department's task of "verify lead time from suppliers on nonstock parts" Serves as an example. Let's assume the department has determined that a request containing one to five part numbers will require one hour, and a request containing more than five part numbers takes two hours on the average. Let us further assume that the department set a goal of keeping the waiting time at three hours or less (instead of the current one-and-a-half days!).

The department finds that when there is a queue of work waiting that totals more than six hours (given its current staff and workload), there is a good probability that the three-hour goal for wait time is in jeopardy (remember that the department can have more than one person simultaneously working on a task). A simple visual in this department can serve to show if there is a problem. First, mark the goal into red, yellow, and green zones. Then create a board with hooks on it, with each hook representing one hour of work. Incoming requests can be put on the hooks according to how many hours of work they represent (see Figure 12-2, reproduced in color on page 27). When too many requests are hung on the board, they enter into the yellow and red zones indicating that the manager must take some action. With any system like the one displayed in Figure 12-2, you need a method to ensure work is handled in a first-in, first-out order.

With these visual indicators, the manager can easily understand the current situation and take some appropriate actions. Several possible responses to the problem are listed below:

- The manager starts to help process the requests.
- The manager reprioritizes tasks for department staff and has them help process the requests.
- The manager asks the staff to work overtime.

Remember not to hide the workload inside in-trays or computers.

Reducing Processing Time

Once you have increased the percentage of complete and accurate orders and reduced the waiting time, you can begin to look into reducing processing time. You should begin with your longest process times, especially any that the team knows are taking too long.

Within each task, you also need to understand any smaller steps. As you examine each step, see whether everyone involved performs the steps in the same sequence and uses the same method. Sometimes, a lack of standardized work is what is causing the task to take too long. Whatever changes you decide to make, document the task with standardized work and train everyone involved.

Following Up with Action Plans from the Workshop

Action plans should be prioritized based on a "impact versus implementation matrix" as shown in Figure 11-4. All action plans should follow a plan-do-check-act cycle. Action plans should also clarify what improvement is expected from the action and, wherever possible, these improvements should be tracked to a specific target. Something similar to the format shown in Figure 12-3 is recommended because it includes elements found in the PDCA cycle.

Processing an order—Action Plan

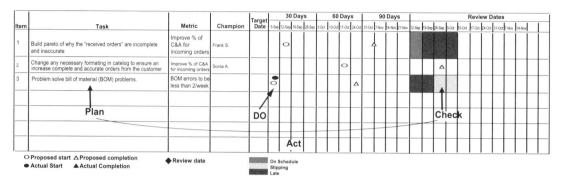

Figure 12-3. Task tracking chart that includes the plan-do-check-act cycle.

Note: A similar task list is shown in color in chapter 1 as part of Figure 1-6.

Having a specific way to measure the success of each action is important. As Figure 12-4, reproduced in color on page 27, shows, the format for tracking can be very simple; a common mistake is not linking the action to a measurable improvement.

Examples of Opportunities During an Office Process Kaizen

The following are a few examples of the improvements you can see once you implement office process kaizen.

Understand a corporate or regulatory agency's requirement. Some activities are performed "because it has always been done that way" or because "it is a regulatory requirement." Further investigation, however, often reveals that nobody is sure where the so-called requirement comes from or exactly what is required. Sometimes, the description of what is really necessary is misunderstood. (Remember, regulatory organizations deal with standards like ISO, which rarely define the exact processes or standards. Instead, they ask the company to define the standard and then check whether the company is following its own rules.)

An example of how big a difference can exist between a requirement and what is perceived to be true about a requirement is a company manufacturing for the British military. The company prints and physically archives all documents related to the parts it manufactures as they assume the military requires this, but the military's actual need is only to have documents kept in a secure database. Printing and physically storing is, therefore, an unnecessary activity.

Calling or sending reminders. Most processes can be automated to have a computer system send e-mail reminders. Instead of chasing suppliers for late orders, for example, the person responsible for monitoring when orders are to arrive sends an automated e-mail a few days before the order is due, asking the supplier to confirm the delivery date.

Summary of Key Points

- Office process kaizen is used to map and improve a specific process that has been identified as needing improvement. If you cannot specifically determine which process to tackle, start with the inputting of an order, or utilize office department kaizen (see chapter 11).

- Many opportunities for improvement can be found in incomplete and inaccurate information, waiting time, and process time.

- The key parts of this process are to quantify the C&A, WT, and PT, and to show these factors in a visual format to help highlight opportunities.

- Standardize where possible; for example, specify where customers should send it, acceptable order formats, and the standard timeframe in which to process an order.

- Eliminate unnecessary steps (i.e., verifying prices when these do not fluctuate, verifying a drawing when no changes have taken place, backing up correspondence with paper copies when you have the electronic records available).

- Put in place (or revise) standardized work for any processes you change.

13

Improving Your Product Costing

Product costing is difficult, but it becomes significantly more so when you have a wide variety of products and a wide range of volumes within those product groups. Major reasons for poor product costing include the following:

- Many costs are allocated inaccurately.
- Overhead allocations are based on volumes or direct labor.
- Direct and indirect labor costs are usually inaccurate.

Allocations (flexibility in determining the distribution of costs) generally cause the greatest inaccuracy in product costing, and inaccurate product costing leads to poor data on which to base decisions. Low-volume businesses have a higher percentage of their costs in overhead (an allocated cost) than do high-volume businesses, making accurate allocations all the more critical.

Compounding the problem is that direct labor, which once consumed the lion's share of product cost, is now usually only 10 percent to 20 percent of a product's cost. Most of today's product cost is in *overhead* (costs to the business that exist regardless of whether products are being produced, for example, rent, mortgage, management salaries, engineers' salaries, and so on), and this has an even greater impact on low-volume plants. Overhead is generally an allocated cost and since direct labor now accounts for a smaller portion of the total cost, the percentage of cost based on allocations is at an all-time high. Thus, by improving the accuracy of allocations you improve the accuracy of any product's actual cost, this should be a primary focus for low-volume businesses. The benefits from good product costing are as follows:

- You can understand the profitability of individual products.
- You have the ability to price products more accurately.

• If you measure the current allocated costs, you can manage them against the standard and understand the deviations.

This chapter does not discuss the differences or reasoning behind market-driven or cost-driven pricing, but focuses on simple ways to improve understanding of the office and production costs associated with your individual products. If you calculate your costs accurately, you can determine your pricing more accurately. The method you use to do so is immaterial. Also note that this discussion does not address how the cost is effected by the order/lot size (therefore set-up times are not addressed) though this is a critical consideration to factor into pricing in low-volume environments.

Product Costing As it Applies to High-Mix, Low-Volume Businesses

Some background information can help clarify why accurate product costing is more difficult in high-mix businesses. A few assumptions used in this discussion are listed below:

• Companies have few products that account for a higher percentage of sales and many low-volume products, each representing only a small portion of the total sales.

• Products vary in work content (both in the office and in production).

• Direct material costs are normally accurate.

• Most of the overhead costs are allocated in one form or another.

Figure 13-1 shows the sales of individual products (A–L) and the cumulative sales line that is typical for a plant with high product variation. Normally, there

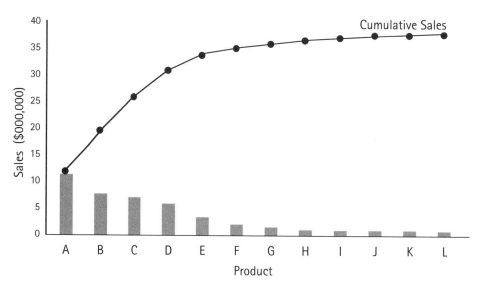

Figure 13-1. Typical sales of higher-volume products compared with a cumulative sales line.

are many more products than those shown in the figure, and the cumulative sales line becomes more or less flat as each additional product accounts for only a small part of total sales volume. The remaining graphs in this chapter also relate to the sales figures of products A–L.

The problems that companies encounter under these or similar conditions are typical:

- Overhead costs are not proportional to direct labor (meaning some products, especially low-volume products, require more overhead or indirect support).
- Indirect labor costs are not relative to sales.
- Costs to process work orders (processing time, preparing documentation, scheduling, changeover, and so on) are not proportional to sales.
- Purchasing, planning, engineering, sales, and management spend a disproportionate amount of time on these low-volume products.
- Direct labor costs are not accurate and not well adjusted to various order sizes.

These problems all lead to inaccurate product costs, which then lead to inaccurate calculations of gross margins, which then lead to faulty decision making. Further problems are caused by traditional accounting:

- Overhead is usually allocated based on volume or direct labor.
- Assets are allocated in a similar way.
- Other general allocations make up most of a product's cost.

Figure 13-2 shows that when overhead is allocated based on direct labor or volume, you are overabsorbing on high-volume products A–E, and underabsorbing on the remaining low-volume products F–L. This is typical with high-mix businesses where processing a small order takes proportionally more time per part with respect to sales, engineering, scheduling, preparing production, shipping, invoicing, and so on. If you allocate these processing (overhead) costs based on direct labor or sales, you allocate proportionally, regardless of whether the product is high- or low-volume. With this approach, the additional time per-part cost is not included in the low-volume product cost calculation. The result is an erroneous impression that there is less profit on high-volume products and more profit on the low-volume products than is actually true. This could lead to increasing sales of low-volume products with incorrect prices and increase the confusion about actual profit margins.

Figure 13-2 is also typical for other allocations like indirect labor, sales costs; asset allocation, and other general, administrative, and corporate costs. These additional allocations intensify the magnitude of the problem faced by low-volume businesses. Also, remember that although the cost of direct labor is

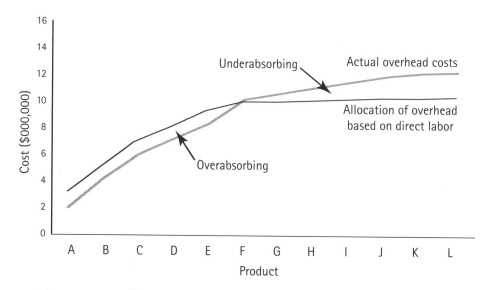

Figure 13-2. Allocation of overhead compared with actual overhead.

estimated or established based on individual products, it is rarely continuously measured and verified, and therefore, rarely accurate. When working on many small orders, operators lose time finding prints, locating tooling, and reacquainting themselves with processes, as do inspectors and other people indirectly involved with the process functions. As a rule, this indirect labor is not measured or factored into the cost. (Methods to calculate direct labor costs more accurately are presented in chapter 3.) Also some low-volume plants do not correctly factor setup time into their price as the manufacturing batch size changes in relation with the order size.

Inaccurate allocations lead to profitability patterns like those shown in Figure 13-3. Notice that at (or near) product F, the total cost increases more quickly than the cumulative sales, which reduces the profit. This is representative of the profit (before taxes) of a high-mix, low-volume business that utilizes significant allocations. The graph might seem extreme, but remember that typically 50 percent to 70 percent of costs (excluding those associated with purchased materials) are allocated, leaving a large margin of error in costing and pricing.

Figure 13-3 shows what typically occurs when profit is made on some of the high-volume products and then lost on the low-volume parts. As the figure indicates, only the first four products (A to D) are profitable. Product E is a breakeven. You start losing profitability on products F through L, and this trend usually continues with any remaining low-volume products.

Solutions for Poor Allocations

If you had any doubts about the magnitude of the problems caused by allocations, it is hoped that the discussion and graphs in the preceding section have

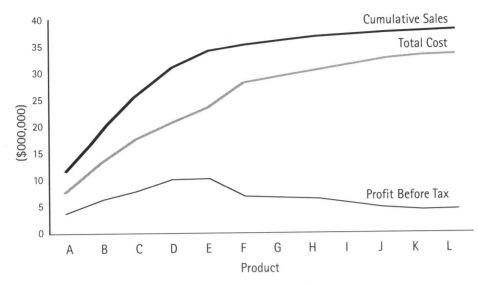

Figure 13-3. Cumulative profit before taxes.

changed your perceptions and even your opinion on this matter and have motivated you to take aggressive action to improve your allocation system. Obviously, this does not mean that you should immediately stop producing products F through L or raise prices (unless you feel the market will accept higher prices). What it does mean is that you should begin to reduce your reliance on allocated costs. The following sections share ways to drive your organization in this direction.

Separating into Value Streams

Separating your shop into two or more value streams, either by product type or by high- and low-volume products, is a great way to discourage allocations. The idea is to manage the complete flow of a product, instead of managing functional departments. Changing to value stream management (as opposed to functionally managing) has numerous advantages. The advantage specifically related to product costing is that value stream managers will need to share common resources from supporting departments (engineering, purchasing, materials) and, therefore, accounting will need to find a new way to allocate costs. Value stream managers will want these costs to be correctly proportioned and charged, so they are encouraged to manage and measure how those resources are used and allocated. Initiating studies that reveal how people in these departments spend their time leads to more accurate costing and, almost always, to improvement opportunities.

Once a manager understands how the time is spent on particular products within each department, he or she can work with the staff to develop a better method to allocate costs more accurately. This will also highlight activities that should be improved.

Traditional departmental managers, on the other hand, are less likely to question overheads as they usually feel that costs are easier to assign directly to a functional department. For example, the assembly manager may assume that most of the purchasing department's time is spent buying vast quantities of materials, when in reality, a greater proportion of the time is spent quoting materials for the sales department's customer quotations. The value stream manager, on the other hand, will likely question why his high-volume products are receiving such high allocations from purchasing (as compared with the low-volume value stream). Sooner than later, this situation will be analyzed, the likely cause will be found, and a costing system more in line with reality than allocations based on direct labor or volume will be implemented.

Measuring Overhead Costs and Using Precise Allocations

If you're not able to utilize value stream managers, measure overhead costs and use precise allocations:

- choose departments that have significantly high allocated costs;
- use time cards or diaries to gather data on how much time is spent on particular products;
- analyze and categorize data;
- develop a method to charge overhead costs based on this data;
- and agree on how this can be done without significantly increasing the accounting department's workload. Also consider conducting office department kaizen with the accounting department to reduce its current workload.

In Figure 13-4, the purchasing department has three buyers and a manager, and the figure shows how the three buyers spend their time during one week. The manager's time is not included, but can be absorbed in the hourly rate. The job numbers denoted with a D are the new-development jobs, and the WO represents work orders. From this data, we can determine that a development job requires an average of 14 hours in purchasing. The work order shows it requires about 6 hours of purchasing time on the average.

We can further take the 21 hours of general commodity purchasing and 9 hours of administrative time and make sure these are absorbed in the purchasing hourly rate.

Assume that to cover all costs of the purchasing manager, commodity purchasing, and administrative time, you have an hourly rate of $55/hour. Thus:

Development job = 14 hours × $55/hour = $770/development job

Work order = 6 hours × $55/hour = $330/work order

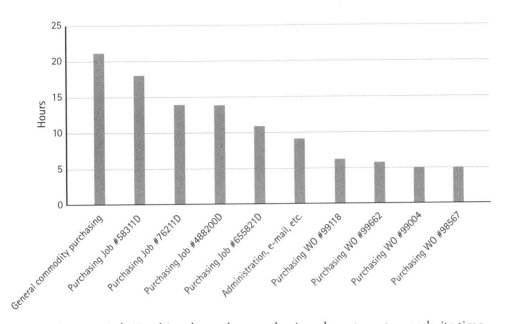

Figure 13-4. Tracking how the purchasing department spends its time.

This department can now apply a specific cost to each job for the purchasing labor based on the type of job rather than using a general allocation.

Performing Office Department Kaizen

Once you find a department that has significantly more time dedicated to tasks than you feel appropriate, or one that is a significant cost driver from the data you have gathered, you can conduct office department kaizen to reduce wasteful procedures or simply eliminate non-value-added time and cost (see chapter 11).

Starting Lean Accounting

Traditional accounting measures financial performance, but many companies use it to measure overall performance, which it was not designed to do. Lean accounting, on the other hand, is a set of performance measures that analyze processes and results. Basically you want activity-based costing because it looks at products as consuming resources. It does not replace traditional accounting but is implemented in incremental steps as lean methods are implemented. The benefits of lean accounting are as follows:

- Increases sales by using value stream costing (true costing with less allocation that is easily understandable) instead of standard costing (which allocates based on rules instead of looking at actual costs incurred); New quotes are more in line with actual cost impacts, and companies are less likely to outsource without good reason (because of full absorption costing)

- Supports that primary purpose of waste elimination (through lean improvements) is to create additional capacity that can be profitably sold
- Reduces internal transactions, for example:
  - Counting inventory, because less material is kept on hand
  - Tracking production status, because this is now monitored on the shop floor

Consider this example without using specific costs: A company I worked with decided to specify engineering costs (accounting for 4 percent of total cost), which were previously rolled into its general labor rate, more accurately. To do this, the company first divided its products into three categories: runners, repeaters, and strangers. Because company managers understood that runners had only engineering costs during startup, they decided to track hours directly and charge high-volume products only at startup. They split the 4 percent into 1.5 percent rolled into the general labor rate for the repeaters and 2.5 percent into the strangers (which require more engineering time).

Although this book does not cover lean accounting extensively, the basics should encourage you to adjust your accounting and performance measures in line with lean accounting as you begin your lean implementation. Many books and experts can provide detailed descriptions of good lean accounting.

Summary of Key Points

- Separate businesses into value streams, by type of product or by high versus low volume and challenge each value stream manager to reduce costs through a better understanding of allocated costs.
- Collect workload data from support departments like purchasing, planning, engineering, sales, and management, and then develop a more precise overhead cost for both high- and low-volume classifications of products.
- Collect workload data from indirect employees for both high- and low-volume products.
- Begin associating a time with each job on the shop floor and verifying it with day-by-hour charts (discussed in chapters 3 and 4).
- Once allocations have been minimized and costs are fully understood, adjust pricing and margins on those products that are not profitable. It is okay to have unprofitable products in a product line as long as you understand which ones they are and how they affect the business.
- Drop unprofitable products (after understanding actual costs)
  - if the market will not accept a price increase;

- if dropping products will not jeopardize customers or sales of associated products;
- if, after applying lean and eliminating waste, you are unable to make them profitable; or
- if engineering is not able to make design changes to quickly reduce the cost.

Conclusions

Some companies implement lean because someone has experienced lean's benefits and understands that lean can improve an entire organization. Others might use lean to help accomplish a specific business goal or go lean because the boss told them to. Whatever has led you to expand your lean knowledge, the general approach to quality, volume, and cost described in this book should always be followed. Indeed, the flow chart in the introduction to this book should be the foundation for your planning a lean strategy.

Once your quality is stable, you want to design a better way to align volume with capacity by putting the appropriate visual management in place. Many lean experts recommend starting with value stream mapping, because this directly helps to improve lead time and flow, which are ways to reduce cost. I suggest that it is better to put good visuals in place as a first step to understanding your current status and drive improvements. Do not forget that you will need to review your metrics and ensure they are driving you in the right direction. It is essential to immediately follow the visualization with a management-auditing system, or the company culture and the habits of those involved will not sustain the visuals.

The next major drive of improvement in high-mix plants is to associate a time with each job, which produces two fundamental benefits: It sets an expectation for production and allows for planning. This drives productivity improvements only when it is properly visualized and monitored through day-by-hour boards or FIFO boards. Once these boards are in place, you should have an immediate productivity improvement and a better understanding of where your true capacity lies. If your company has let slip any monitoring of your productivity, you need to refocus it with the methods presented in this book.

Once you are tracking and monitoring productivity, you can begin using various lean tools, depending on whether you are short of capacity or have excess capacity. Using day-by-hour boards, SMED, bottleneck analysis, OEE, standardized work, and other tools will allow you to increase your capacity. Skills matrices, rationalizing machinery, and workload smoothing will help if you have excess capacity or need to create more flexible capacity for the future.

After your volume is better balanced to capacity, you can use value stream mapping to identify many types of opportunities, especially those related to reducing lead time and cost. Through the symbols and data presented in the mapping, you can identify many opportunities, decide on which area you will concentrate, and then quantify your expectations on a future state value stream map. One area that will offer opportunities will be your inventory; you'll need to push and flow instead of pulling material. Kanban systems can be successfully implemented in high-mix, low-volume plants when combining them with MRP: a hybrid pull/push system.

Manpower improvements and machine productivity opportunities are also critical in reducing costs. Improving manpower includes better workplace organization, implementing standardized work, and visualizing repetitive parts on an operator balance wall. You also need cross-trained team members, teamwork, and motion kaizen, which can be used for your higher volume tasks. Also put in place machine and operator andon systems. Better machine performance comes from understanding your OEE and deciding where to put your efforts; for example, focusing on TPM, machine kaizen, and/or the balance between shift patterns. Finally, you are ready to look at your layout and at flow through your plant to see what opportunities exist for rearranging your processes.

Because low-volume plants have a higher portion of their workforce performing office functions, such as procuring materials, planning, designing, and supporting those many small orders, the office offers many opportunities for improvement in administrative and support functions. Identify whether you have an entire department with significant opportunities or a particular process (like processing an order) that offers opportunities. Then hold an office department kaizen or an office process kaizen.

No less critical is your approach to product costing. Because many costs are allocated, you may not be costing products correctly or know your actual profit per product. Better costing (by utilizing fewer allocations) is easier after implementing value stream management, visual management, standardized work, or office department kaizen.

For lean to succeed, everyone's habits and behavior must change. In particular, management's behavior must change from managing by reports presented in meeting rooms to managing from the shop floor with visuals in real time. Keep in mind that none of the tools presented in this book should be used as permanent solutions, instead they should be temporary measures until something better is found. Make sure you have correct measurement systems in place and a metric for productivity and lead time. Focus all your improvements on non-value-added activities first.

Glossary

andon A visual (and normally audio) communication system that notifies everyone of abnormalities or that support is required. This can be activated manually or automatically by a machine.

BOM (bill of material) A structured list for a semi-finished or finished product that lists all the component parts, with the names, reference numbers, quantities, and units of measure of each component necessary to complete the product.

day-by-hour board A visual scheduling board that relates the production schedules to required processing time for the processes and allows for real-time status tracking.

FIFO (first in, first out) A queue in which the first item coming into the queue is handled first, the next one coming in is handled second, and so on.

job shop A manufacturer that might have only one production run before the part or revision changes. It is unknown whether or when there may be further orders for that particular part. Normally, a job shop is not responsible for design of the products but manufactures to customers' specifications.

kaizen To make good changes in the form of continuous improvements.

kanban A signaling system based on consumption, which is set up to replace what the "customer" takes. It is a type of pull system.

low volume Products that are produced in small volumes and batches (usually far less than 100 parts per batch). In some cases, the customer may forecast the usage or the production period.

MRP (materials requirements planning) A just-in-time tool that helps materials (purchased or internally produced) arrive just when they are required. It also is used to plan for capacity and human resources.

OEE (overall equipment effectiveness) A standard machine performance measurement that encompasses all losses not contributing to good parts on a machine or process. It is equal to the combined effect of availability $\times$ performance $\times$ quality.

Pareto chart Chart used to graphically summarize and display the relative importance of the differences between groups of data. It is normally a bar chart displaying the data in descending order, and it shows the cumulative percentage as a line so that everyone is aware of the overall impact of each additional category.

PDCA (plan-do-check-act) A model that provides a framework for the improvement of a process or system. It can be used to monitor a single task or guide an entire improvement project.

ROI (return on investment) For a given amount of money, how much profit or cost savings are realized.

SMED (single minute exchange of dies) The process of reducing changeover (setup) time by classifying elements as internal or external to a machine's operating time and then converting the internal elements so they can be done externally (while the machine continues to operate).

TPM (total productive maintenance) The process of stabilizing equipment, thereby increasing availability, performance, and quality.

WIP (work-in-process) An asset representing the portion of work that is complete but not yet billed. WIP assets are goods at various stages of completion throughout the plant, from raw material that has been released for initial processing to completely processed material awaiting final inspection until it is accepted as finished goods inventory.

Index

About the Author

Greg Lane earned his master of business administration from California State University in 1989 and his bachelor of science in mechanical engineering from the University of Wisconsin in 1986. He is a faculty member of the Lean Enterprise Institute.

While working with Toyota, Greg was one of a handful of candidates selected for a one-year training program conducted by Toyota's masters. He became a Toyota Production System (TPS) Key Person and continued his work with Toyota by training others in TPS.

Since 1992, he has been working on implementing lean around the world, supporting large and small companies alike. In 1998, he began to refocus his lean endeavors on meeting the specific needs of high-mix, low-volume enterprises. Although his work is geared to companywide improvements, Greg has also worked with individual departments—purchasing, engineering, finance, planning—to improve efficiencies, reduce lead times, and reduce costs.

During his time as an independent consultant, Greg purchased and operated (for almost six years) his own manufacturing company, which specialized in fast turnaround on high-mix, low-volume parts. Greg used TPS to grow the business and nearly double its sales. He sold the business at a profit to concentrate on supporting others in lean implementation.

Greg and his associates have experience not only at adapting the methods contained in this book, but also in applying other tools that are too numerous to detail here. He can be reached for further support with your lean transformation by e-mailing *BecomeLean@aol.com* or directing your web browser to *www.LowVolumeLean.com*.